HAUNTINGS
IN LINCOLNSHIRE

HAUNTINGS
IN LINCOLNSHIRE

Tales of the everyday paranormal

STEPHEN WADE

HALSGROVE

British Library Cataloguing-in-Publication Data
A CIP record for this title is available from the British Library

ISBN 978 1 84114 894 6

HALSGROVE
Halsgrove House,
Ryelands Industrial Estate,
Bagley Road, Wellington, Somerset TA21 9PZ
Tel: 01823 653777   Fax: 01823 216796
email: sales@halsgrove.com

Part of the Halsgrove group of companies
Information on all Halsgrove titles is available at: www.halsgrove.com

Printed and bound by Short Run Press, Exeter

CONTENTS

ACKNOWLEDGEMENTS

Writing a collection of haunting tales requires all kinds of contacts and sources, and half the pleasure of writing these tales is in sifting the reliable from the marginal. Experts and enthusiasts have made this task easier.

Much of the source material has been partial and piecemeal, but odd scraps of information have meant that experiences may be checked and verified in broader reference books; but it has to be said that the oral recall of experience is integral to most of the stories in the book.

I would like to thank Mary Payne and the good people of Scunthorpe and Epworth who told me some rare tales, particularly John Bowers, Hazel, Tom Short, Derrick Kinsley, the Antcliff family and Keith at the Old School House. Thanks are due also to Edward Dodd, local writer on Brigg; also I have to acknowledge earlier research by Jared Williams and David Lightfoot, and to Amy and Chris Wade for some of the artwork.

Thanks also go to the various investigation groups who have reported their activities and findings, both in the local press and on the internet. Without these organisations of enthusiasts, there would be very little up-dating of the stories set solidly in the usual collections of long-established tales.

Staff at Lincoln Central Libraries have been very helpful, and Ged Payne at the Illustrations Index, Lincolnshire Archives, has been unfailingly kind in supplying illustrations of Harlaxton Manor and Thorpe Hall. Appeals for stories were broadcast on BBC Radio Lincolnshire, printed in *Lincolnshire Life*, and in Sarah Holt's feature in *The Lincolnshire Echo* in October, 2008. Thanks to these outlets for helping to access some stories from people across the county.

John Ketteringham's *Lincolnshire Hotchpotch* provided some interesting sidelights on some established tales, particularly on the vicar of Caistor and on Bolingbroke Castle. When it comes to related discussion groups and short reports, the sources are too numerous to mention.

Helen and Paul brought together some excellent stories, and these are included here: thanks to them.

Finally, I owe much gratitude to the various correspondents, named and anonymous, who have sent accounts of their paranormal experience, particularly Bev Butcher, who took time to write to me. The unexplained is very much *dead and alive* in Lincolnshire.

Picture credits:
The pictures, where indicated, are from the Local Studies collection, Lincoln Central Library and Lincolnshire Archives, by courtesy of Lincolnshire County Council, Education and Cultural Services Directorate.

Other illustrations are from the author's collection.

INTRODUCTION

Lincolnshire, the Yellowbelly county, is long and broad. Driving across its expanse, it may appear monotonous because there is so much farming there: it is a workmanlike place, with a charm and beauty of its own. The visitor who approaches but who does not really take note will miss the subtle contrasts. These are more than simply the Fens in the south and the Wolds down the spine. The escarpment that follows the path of the Roman road from Scunthorpe down to south of Lincoln gives a wonderful view across to the Midlands, and in the north of the county, between the Isle of Axholme and Grimsby, you are never far away from the magnificent breadth and grandeur of the Humber estuary.

As is so often the case, the most unusual places in the county are often hidden away down lanes, in the dip of a wold, or in a spinney across several broad fields. Lincolnshire is a place of villages and churches in abundance. It has often been said that 'as sure as God's in Lincolnshire…' is a very meaningful oath. There are church spires in every vista. Where there are silent places, there are stories of hauntings. Where there has been turbulent history, there are spectres displaced and disturbed, and the city of Lincoln has ghosts around every street corner, in cellars, attics, castle grounds and in old shops. It has been visited by television mediums and researchers, including *Derek Acorah's Ghost Towns*, and the focus is usually Steep Hill – a place absolutely packed with ghostly tales.

Lincoln itself has seen violent history; in the Medieval period it was often the centre of massive political and military confrontations; but also the wider cultural heritage has brought its stories, passed down in oral tradition as well as in the books. Tom Otter's ghost still moves around, they say, close by the spot where he was gibbeted after killing his new wife, and some dark spirit loiters in the Victorian prison on Greetwell Road, where felons were hanged. Even the car park by the castle is a place with a terrible past: the tower by Cobb Hall was a hanging place when execution in this country was a spectator sport, and now that the huge trees have been cleared from the slope beneath the walls and towers, the modern pedestrian can imagine the popular hanging days when people paid money for a seat in the nearest tavern for a prime view of the neck-stretching. In the house to the left of the castle entrance as one walks in, the attic room was where the famous hangman, William Marwood, used to stay when he came to town to officiate at a nasty judicial killing.

Daniel Defoe, touring the country in the 1720s, wrote, 'Here within land we see Brigg, Caistor, Louth, Horncastle, Bolingbroke, Spilsby, Wainfleet and Boston. As these are all, except the last, inland towns, they afford nothing remarkable...' How wrong can a man be: even a great writer like Defoe. These places have their rich, complex stories in their long history, and many of these events and people of the past have permeated the fabric of modern life today, making themselves known by sight, sound, smell and touch, in all the everyday lives of Lincolnshire folk. As with all travel, there is an encounter with the mysterious past as well as the demanding present, and these tales will show how past time somehow interweaves with our lives.

But my stories range across the whole county, so we also visit Epworth, home of the Wesleys, in the north, a place also overflowing with paranormal happenings, and the steel town of Scunthorpe has its share of the unexplained too. In my notebook of investigations I have three tales from Scunthorpe all from private houses, and I include these in my conclusions as I have experienced these at first hand.

The stories here from Lincolnshire tend to have a bias towards Lincoln itself, but each area has its own appeal in terms of its unexplained narratives

North Lincolnshire has its own peculiar beauty, perhaps most patently so in winter, when the low fields you might see as you drive along the M180 are folded in a spectral mist, and the bare trees are trimmed in glistening frost. But as night falls, it is also a place of fog, of seemingly endless country lanes, and few notable landmarks. In such a place, travellers might easily lose their way. In the midnight fog they might also fancy they see spirits on the road, or figures haunting the lone trees and the shadows of the hedges. But these stories also show that most ghostly presences appear within four walls, often pubs or shops. In Gainsborough, one ghostly visitor shocked a whole bunch of macho firefighters. Another figure is Old Tom of Epworth, quite matey, but still from the next world, sending a chill into the room. I hope you find some interest here, and some tales to send you out ghost-hunting. The fact is, they seem to find us, and usually when we least expect to see them.

TALES FROM NORTH LINCOLNSHIRE

Old Tom the Friendly Ghost

Epworth

Some houses have moods; they may be dark or light. In this story, the house is a home to something whimsical, something with the habits of a sprite. But the presence is very human, very cosy, and all too unpredictable.

The attractive village of Epworth, home of the Wesleys, figures in most books concerned with ghostly appearances, mainly because the ghost of Old Jeffrey in the rectory is documented in several standard accounts of the Wesley family and their 'banging ghost' – a poltergeist active around 1716.

The village seems to be a focus for ghostly activity. The pubs and offices have their share of stories, but there is one private dwelling, existing for three centuries but having had only three occupants, that has a very definite otherworldly entity inside its walls. Comfortingly, though, it is quite amiable and has never done anything menacing or wicked.

At number 27, New Street, Epworth, the Antcliff family have grown accustomed to living with their own personal ghost. He is almost a member of the family, and they call him Old Tom. During excavation for building work behind the property, the family found a gravestone with the name Tom Rivington carved on it, and just one date decipherable: 1887. So, their invisible guest became Old Tom.

The children of the family have experienced some of the most definite appearances of the old man; the son recalls that, lying in bed one night, he sensed someone getting into bed beside him. He felt the pressure of the bed taking the weight, and a sense of a body pressing gently on him. The bedrooms seem to be Tom's favourite places to join in with family life: Mrs Antcliff recalls being in bed when something patted the edge of the bed, as if feeling in the dark, and then touched her in a sensitive place.

Epworth Rectory.

Old Tom has been known to kick the dog, and send him scurrying into a dark corner; he has walked across the floor between one bedroom and the bathroom, and his footsteps can often be heard treading across the floor as the family sit down to tea. He specialises in moving from an area which previously contained a large corner cupboard to a room upstairs. A small area at the foot of the stairs is constantly very cold, despite the absence of any source of draughts.

The most noisy and substantial activity came one evening when the family sat down to their evening meal. The kitchen is spacious, with plenty of room for the people and their pets – a dog and a budgie. There are high shelves around the room, and as they sat at table, the youngest daughter's school lunch-box, placed high up but behind a wooden lip at the top of a cupboard, suddenly sprang into the air and seemed to be hurled across the room – and this at the very moment the mother spoke about it.

This was quite early in the Antcliff's life with Old Tom. It was highly disturbing, but nothing to cause real apprehension followed this for some time. It was a case of Old Tom being there, carrying on as 'normal.' Mrs Antcliff recalls often hearing her daughters, when alone upstairs, talking to someone. Being asked who was there, they would say, 'the old man again…'

Maybe the sociable guest from the other side is Tom Rivington, and his spirit doesn't want to leave the place he loved in this life. The Antcliffs are not concerned. The worst he has done is pat someone's backside and kick the dog.

But there is one interesting coda to this tale. On the night of my visit, I sat in the kitchen asking questions, and I was startled by the sudden chirp of a bird. It was the budgie in the corner, bouncing around in his small cage. I laughed, and said, without thinking, 'Hey Billy… you made me jump!' Mrs Antcliff asked me, with some amazement, how I knew its name.

I had no idea how I knew. Maybe Old Tom was prompting me, for some mischief.

'Let the Devil Flee From Me!'

Epworth Rectory

In John Wesley's short memoir of the hauntings at Epworth Rectory, written in 1784, he ends with his father's response to a call from friends that he should leave his home: 'No, let the devil flee from me: I will never flee from the devil!' Soon after, the paranormal activities ceased.

To visit the rectory now is to experience peace and withdrawal from the troubles of the world. A tour around the rooms, even the attic where a certain spirit called Old Jeffrey was supposedly active, is to feel relaxed, and somehow taken back to quieter times. The place is just off the Gainsborough road, south of Epworth, an easy walk from the market square of the town, and you walk past the memorial statue of John Wesley as you do so.

But in the years around 1716-1719, there is enough evidence to suggest that the rectory certainly had a noisy and frightening poltergeist. John's account, based on questioning of family and servants in the year 1720, relates tales of knockings, objects being moved and even the family mastiff dog being so scared that it cowered and ran for cover by the side of John's parents.

So familiar were these unexplained happenings that the large family gradually began to be familiar with the process of the hauntings. John relates that his sisters became attuned to the knocks and sounds. After hearing knocks on their bed-head, they would say that Jeffrey was coming, and that it was time to go to sleep. But it must have been no joke, in those tiny, ill-lit rooms and corridors, to feel that there could be an emanation at any time – and in any one of the many rooms. For instance, nothing had happened in John's father's study until one night when he went into his room and the door slammed open so violently that it shook him and almost knocked him to the floor.

Mr Wesley repeatedly tried to address the poltergeist, sometimes feeling that it was the spirit of his dead son, Samuel, and at other times, being sure that it was a malevolent sprite. On one occasion he said to the ghoul: 'Thou deaf and dumb devil, why dost though fright these children, that cannot answer thee themselves?' In response came a familiar knocking, and then some hours of peace from its torments.

Trouble seems to have started in 1716, when a servant, Robert Brown, was sitting resting in the late evening. He and a maid heard knocking at the door and when opened, there was nobody to be seen. But when poor Robert went to his bed, he saw in front of him, in the garret, a hand-mill whirling in the air. The session of torture from the other world ended with the ghost making the sound of a turkey-cock by the unfortunate Robert's bed-side.

There seems to have been a hex on the building. When the place was on fire in 1709, and people thought that everyone had been brought out to safety, the outline of a boy was spotted upstairs and he was thereupon rescued too. The boy was no less than John Wesley himself. So at least there is some small piece of good fortune in this troublesome tale in Epworth's Rectory, now a tourist destination.

Old Jeffrey, as he came to be called, was called so by Emily, one of the Wesley daughters. She discovered that an old man had died there, and that this restless soul was probably him. One of the most intriguing aspects of the haunting is the fact that activity was more marked when family prayers were occasionally not spoken; what that tells us remains a mystery, but the one certain fact is the attic where Jeffrey is supposed to have focused his nuisances and terror is still rather bare and unnaturally silent. You feel an atmosphere as you walk in, even today. Though a peaceful place, the rectory may still have some residual energy from Jeffrey and his nasty tricks.

A steady walk through Epworth, stopping off at the Red Lion where

John used to sit sometimes, then past the high walls by the side of the through-road, gives the visitor no idea of the former restless ghost who roamed that area, and who terrorised the Wesley family for so long. But in the end, Mr Wesley would not 'flee'.

Old School House Tales

Set back from one of the winding streets of Epworth, the Old School House is a red-brick building with an attractive, spacious feel to it. Nothing in the outward appearance suggests what things go on inside those walls.

Some say that Epworth is at the junction of ley-lines. Locals will tell you of murders and foul deeds done in those streets and fields, and it certainly is a place with a fascinating and eventful past. There appear to be clusters of ghostly activity in some areas of the town, and surely one of the most puzzling is the history of the Old School House. This is now a public house and restaurant, but it was a school house in days gone by, and that may be a clue to some of the unexplained events within its walls.

The most startling tale is of the school photograph for 1947. The walls of the main lounge bar are lined with old black and white photographs of former classes at the school. Imagine the typical small village school, with a student population of around forty, and you picture the scene. Now, of these dozens of dark photos lining the walls, the picture for 1947 shows three lines of boys, and one of them has no face. His face is blurred, but not scratched out: it is a blur as if he was moving at the time and the image was ruined. But the locals will tell you that the young man who killed himself some years after this photo was this same boy – and the face was blurred after his death.

In the Old School House, there are almost daily occurrences that are beyond explanation. Bar staff are nipped and shoved. Chairs move; figures are seen at tables when the place is closed. One barman, who had worked there for many years, found that pulling a pint one day, some force was pushing against him, and he had to use all his considerable strength to pull the full pint. Is there some tee-totaller at work there? Maybe one of the former teachers, still keeping the local people on the straight and narrow path of the clean-living life?

Another tale defies explanation. Only recently, in 2003, the computer at the central offices of the brewery registered the pumps being used to produce twenty pints of ale in the early hours of one spring morning. The landlord tells the tale with a tone of mystery and disbelief. There had been no late-night drinking and no private party. Yet he could find no trace of glasses being use, nor of any spillage of drink that night.

Someone or something had consumed twenty pints of beer and the computer at the brewery had logged it. We will never know the answer to this. Stories of the supernatural go on being generated at the Old School House. Some presence there wants to make life uneasy for the staff, and sometimes for the visitors.

Legless but not Drunk Spectre in Scunthorpe

If you walk down Scotter Road from the broad roundabout at the Berkeley Hotel in Scunthorpe, you come to a tall viaduct, part of the main railway line from Scunthorpe to Doncaster. At the side of the slope there is a track, a leafy lane, and it leads to open fields on the left-hand side, all the way to Gunness and Keadby Bridge.

No-one visiting Glanford Park football ground, or strolling along the footpath for those few miles would know the horrific spectral appearance often reported by those cornfields: the figure of a legless woman, walking with children.

Many local people have reported seeing this terrifying figure. In 1965, for example, two young men were bird-nesting along there on a bright day in summer. They had no care in the world, and they felt the wonderful sense of freedom the young experience when they are away from routine and out of the four walls of home. They were in nature's realm, but what they saw as they started walking on this lane was horrendously disturbing.

Suddenly they became aware of someone walking ahead of them: a family group strolling by the high yellow corn. The figures were about fifty yards in front, and were by a drainage ditch. One of the boys reported that the woman was wearing a blue dress and had fair hair. There were two young children skipping and dancing in front of her. But what was unreal was the fact that she had no legs.

One of the witnesses to this macabre sight rang a local farmer one day and asked if he had seen anything similar. The tale was told then that a man in Gunness, just a mile or so away, had murdered his wife back in 1927, and that the poor woman's restless spirit walks only reliving her happiest time on earth, in that shimmering, radiant summer in the inter-war years.

Another witness to this ghost tells of a day when he saw the woman walk from the centre of a field, this time alone; she was carrying something, possibly a picnic basket, and again there were happy laughing children. 'Actually, I shouted good morning to them, but they made no response,' he reported. Whoever she was, or is, she is fond of that field, in the open land between Scunthorpe and Gunness, a haven of quiteness between a motorway and the main road to Doncaster. If you walk that way one Sunday on a gentle stroll, watch out for her, and listen for the chuckle of happy children. But they won't notice you.

Disturbances at the Brocklesby Ox

Brigg is a place with a deceptively quiet and workmanlike image. But beneath the market-town bustle and the traffic rumbling around the new by-pass, there is some history, and very strange it is at times. Sometimes supernatural in fact, like the haunting of a particular pub.

As the new landlord, Rob White, says, the Brocklesby Ox pub in Brigg is a 'nice cosy, homely pub with a warm atmosphere, a real fire and good local characters.' But the place, dating from the 1600s, has a long history of spiritual presences and many inexplicable events. The place is named after a beast of some local renown, said to have weighed an immense three tons (the average weight being nearer one ton for such an animal), and it used to be in the hands of the celebrated Pelham family. The first landlord we know about who had the place was one William Foley, in 1835, and uncanny events have been happening ever since.

Mr White had run a public house before – the Sloop in Beverley – and he was looking forward to taking over a friendly place near his home town of Scunthorpe. He must have absorbed the atmosphere, though, as soon as he entered the place. It is old, full of atmosphere and objects from the Brigg agricultural past: a market town in the middle of an area resonant with the folk life of the English shire – the song 'Brigg Fair' has made the village famous, and the first singer of that song, Joseph Taylor, was from a few miles down the road at Saxby. A walk through old Brigg is one of seeing the past through the old pubs along the main street.

Accounts of ghostly hauntings in places of alcoholic refreshment are, of course, always open to the obvious criticisms by sceptics and doubting

Thomases. But there is no doubt that people have seen and felt very disturbing phenomena in 'the Ox'. One of the people with most first-hand knowledge is a cellarman, Tommy Simm, who talks about being lifted and moved while asleep, with some inconceivable force shifting him across the room and dropping him on a rug. 'I was picked up in one place and put down on another' he remembers. This happened in one of the old bedrooms, and he recalls that all he did was blandly return to his bed.

Mr Simm insists that he was not affected by drink on this occasion, and he says that in his seven years of work at the Ox he has had three notable encounters with this mischievous being. The landlord is unperturbed, however, noting that we have more to fear from the living than from the dead, in spite of many instances in which objects as well as people have apparently been moved without any noticeable force on them. But one has to admire the fact that Mr White and Mr Simm have not been afraid to tell their tales; and it may be that, as the old adage has it, 'in wine there is truth spoken.'

The small town of Brigg has its charms: plenty of 'old England' is there when you stop to explore its social history. Even today there is still the annual horse-fair, and a contemplation of the inn-yard of the Angel Hotel (when it was flourishing there) makes you think of travelling players and a society dependent on the horse. But it is also a place with a long history of unexplained events and visitations.

So spend a little time in the Ox but be prepared for a surprise visitor. It might be advisable to ask some of the locals first, so that you might be fore-warned. Maybe there is strength in numbers, but like Mr Simm, you could still be taken over and given a shock, when you least expect it. After all, it's a famous market town, and who knows what odd creatures have been brought into the place and left there, to do some mischief.

The Ghost in the Main Street Shop

Number 56, Wrawby Street, Brigg, is a place to avoid if you want a peaceful life. Many residents of the house and shop over the years have reported seeing and feeling very disturbing events in those walls. The focus of the stories is the spectre of an old man, a small man wearing dark-coloured clothes, and he does not appear to be a benevolent ghost at all. In fact, he leaves people with bad dreams.

The earliest stories of the place start with memories from Marian Kitwood, who was born there in 1913. Her father started a fishmonger's shop there, and he was also a bookmaker. The story about the unwanted visitor is that he is most likely the ghost of a man who hanged himself from one of the bannisters. He had been living in one of the highest rooms in the property.

Marian has spoken about her bad memories there, and also those of her sisters: a bed was moved; they heard footsteps, and a set of service bells used to sound without any human use. She recalls that most of the time, they were not connected to a power supply, yet their ringing was still heard.

She had a little dog, a Pomeranian, and it would never go upstairs and certainly never sleep in her room, which she wanted it to do, just for some company in that atmosphere of dread. The dog refused even to go upstairs at all. Marian was told to stop inventing things and to pull herself together – a common reaction when children report uncanny events to adults, of course.

But the saga goes on: later residents of number 56 continue to tell disturbing stories. Marian's daughter, Janet Murphy, has spoken to a writer about her own experiences there. These include a memory of going downstairs very late at night, and when explaining why she did, said that a small old man had led her down. Janet also recalls seeing a figure on the stairs, a shadowy shape which defied explanation when she was asked to explain what she had seen later.

When the place became a fish and chip shop, strange events multiplied; there were often sounds heard in the upstairs room and on investigation, there was no-one found there. This dates from 1964 when the place was owned by Jack and Florence Wattam. Florence felt a sense of unease from the very start of her time there, and recalls that typical happenings were bread buns just floating in the air and chairs and cutlery being moved.

Strangest of all must be the sight of a little man with a hump-back coming from a cupboard. She describes the sight as shadowy, like a cloud of smoke. But she is clear that the outline figure she saw was a small man wearing a round hat. Amazingly, the figure floated out through a letter-box.

Who knows what is there now, just off the main street, a street that used to be thronged with traffic and shoppers. Who knows who or what loiters in the upper areas of that building. It may well be the restless spirit of the hanged man.

The White Lady and the Watercolour

Many in the beautiful little Lincolnshire village of Hibaldstow have seen her as she walks across a landing or through a yard. She is the White Lady to the residents of the row of eighteenth century cottages, and the only evidence they have of her existence in this life is a gravestone behind a fireplace.

There are four adjoining cottages, once inhabited by labourers working at a nearby dairy; I spoke to three people here, and all have seen or felt a presence in their homes. Some years ago, during renovations, the gravestone was found, and all it had was a name and a date. Now even that is forgotten as the stone was replaced behind the hearth and a new person moved in. But she walks, and she has been seen.

In The White House, once a tavern and also a lock-up with a resident constable, the present owner saw her in the early hours of one morning last year. As he walked in the half-light across a small landing, there she was, looking at him. He describes a filmy shape, with a darker shade at the heart, and a discernible face, sweet and lovely, seeming to look through him. There has been a séance, and the people were given the name 'Florry'. At other times, her figure has been seen but seemingly 'with no legs', so supporting the view that the development of the house, over the years, has meant alterations to levels on which people move.

The White House has also been a place of some poltergeist activity; early one morning a cabinet full of pottery and silverware shook, and the only object to have been dislodged was one newly bought for an aunt – a high quality commemorative plate. Silhouettes of human shapes are often seen and at times the presence of a distinctive and repellent smell lingers by the log basket near the fire.

Something about Hibaldstow (in Old English 'the place of Hubald') attracts spirits from the other side. In this same street there have been sightings of four different entities, as they walk across the closely-knit back gardens. An old man with a pipe has been seen several times, and his tobacco-smoke is often sensed around the garden.

But most amazing of all was my own experience of the watercolour. I was taken to a small bedroom in which, the owner tells me, she has often heard movements and voices above her as she sits in the kitchen below. She took me to see this room, and as we entered she pointed out a watercolour to the right of the door. This was a Victorian painting showing a stone gateway surrounded by dark foliage, and to the lower right of this was the only light area of the picture, showing flagstones with moonlight upon them.

She then told me about the voices in the room, and her family's sightings of two men moving around the house. We spoke about this, and I was aware of nothing unusual, but then she asked me to look again at the painting. To my amazement, the picture was now suffused with light, as if colour had stolen into the vegetation as it would in the real world. I was stunned, and immediately lifted the painting off the wall, to look behind. There was no trick. It was as if the leaves and branches had been suddenly stroked by rays of the sun, and night had turned to day. All I saw behind was a sheet of cardboard and the name K. E. Halket. I have not found this name in any reference work on Victorian painters.

I was told by the owner of the house that the painting was given to her by 'a Quaker lady' who said it would help her retain her faith. Apparently, the painting does these changes almost every week, but never when taken to any other residence.

Everything about this Hibaldstow tale is full of mystery: who was the Quaker lady? Who wanders around the back gardens of the cottages leaving the smell of tobacco? More intriguing is who the two men were in that back bedroom upstairs – men seen and heard by the daughters of the house? The small black cat who lives there seems unperturbed by these events, but who knows what inhabits that mysterious painting?

The houses are very old. The street itself has a sense of timelessness. All the stories of the atmosphere around the dairymen's cottages suggest a little world that comes alive in the dark, only 'alive' may not be the right word to use. More likely, there are creatures wandering the corridors and crossing the landings who were living beings many, many years ago and cannot leave the village today.

There is a long and intriguing history here, of the White Lady and of the watercolour. We may only have a clue if and when the hearthstone is dug out and there is a name. Meanwhile, she walks at early dawn and chooses to be seen at times, perhaps having something to communicate about that quiet lane in Lincolnshire where the small cottages huddle together, near a stables and a farm.

All I know is that I saw the watercolour change in front of me; I saw the dark landscape suffused with a glorious light that had not been there a few minutes earlier. If there is an explanation for these things, they defy science. My visit there is dominated by a black cat, a sense of being watched, and a small piece of canvas on a wall that appears to have defied the normal rules of what we call 'reality'.

Footsteps in the Fire Station

In the course of researching some Lincolnshire ghost experiences, I answered a phone-call one night, and was told this tale.

This is a tale of a homely, restful work-break being torn apart by unexplained movement, unnerving noise, and a mysterious evening guest: some being from the worlds beyond perhaps, but certainly something unexplained, and an experience that has lived in the mind of an old man to this day, as he told me the story.

Back in 1947, when men were leaving the RAF and looking for work, one of the attractions was to enrol in the Fire Service. But those who started work at the Gainsborough station in Lord Street, might have regretted the decision. Former firemen have told me eerie tales of working in that place.

The old appliance room was all that was left of the original building, and it was the custom of the officers to go through the ritual of essential tasks before sitting down to socialise and listen to the radio. The last job of the day was to lock the side door. There was an external alarm bell for the general public to ring if an emergency arose.

One officer recalls that, during the social time, when their kit was hung on the wall, one man was making a model galleon, and the largest piece of wood, about a foot long, was thrown inexplicably across the room, slamming into the opposite wall. But then, footsteps were heard outside and approaching the side door. Everyone heard the footsteps as they were talking, and they seemed to come into the building. The Sub Officer accused a man of not locking the door, but they all walked to see what was going on.

The loud footfalls came into the main room, and then slowly padded along the stone slabs of the corridor. The officers followed, in awe of what they all heard. On the steps went, across a yard and up some steps to a locked store-room which had dangerous substances in it. The officers were, naturally, shaking with fear. Their heads turned, and they felt the floor shake slightly to the sound of these ghostly footsteps, across the room, slowly up the stairs, and then the handle on the door was rattled.

Big, strong men, fearless against the terrors of fire and smoke, shivered with fear that night, roused from a friendly game of dominoes and the homely sound of the radio, to witness something uncanny.

But it seems that Lord Street has even more ghostly activity. One man who lived behind a greengrocer's shop three doors along from the fire station remembers some uncanny events there. He talks of a long passage leading to the outside door, and that he and his wife started to hear loud rappings on this door. Local police would sometimes call in for a cuppa, so they had a chance to talk about their concerns. When the door was opened, there was never anyone there.

Until one night, when the bangings were particularly loud. The man opened the door, and to his horror, the noises continued, all around him, even without the door there, where the banging took place. This became a regular part of life in the house, and to make things worse, there was an upper floor above the people living behind the shop, and often they heard steps above them in the empty room. The man eventually nailed battens across the stairs to block the exit and entrance to the upper floor.

It seems that Lord Street and the nearby Casket Street had (and maybe still have) their share of beings from the other world, and one in particular who likes to walk into dangerous places. People asked about these experiences have no explanation from history, but there is much still to be unearthed about the footfalls in the fire station.

Alkborough Tales

This village seems to be a place that attracts ghosts and spectres. People tell all kinds of strange tales about the place. In the woods nearby, many local people have spotted a white-haired man on a horse, and in the 1950s some gravestones were thrown in a pond. If you wanted to upset the dead, what worse thing could you do? So it comes as no surprise that there are wandering, tormented spirits around there.

One of these is Old Marmaduke on the Burton Road. He has often been seen: a figure from another time, shocking passers-by with the clarity of the appearance: white-haired, dressed in quite fancy clothes and smiling. A benevolent ghost, but still unnerving when seen. We're not clear who christened the old man with this name, but he appears to be a familiar sight. Many roadside wandering figures are seen around the village; he is the most famous.

Local writer, John Bowers, tells this Alkborough tale. It concerns two sisters, both married and with families, but living over a hundred miles apart. Shelley Burton lived in Alkborough, and she had a golden labrador as a family pet. The uncanny tale begins when they bought another dog as a companion for this animal.

When Tracy Burdass (née Bowers) was walking her dog in Cambridge, her sleepy daughter muttered something about Aunty Shelley 'having another dog…'

When told that Aunt Shelley had just one dog, Magnum, the child replied, 'No mummy… they've two dogs!'

That night, as the sisters spoke on the phone, it emerged that the Alkborough Bowers did indeed have a new dog, a black labrador called Pip. When Sophie's mum asked her daughter about this new arrival so far away and whether she knew its colour, the little girl said, without hesitation, 'It's black!'

The Steelworks' Ghost

Surprisingly, there are not so many uncanny stories about the Scunthorpe steelworks, or, if there are, then they have not been widely circulated. But this is one that the person involved recalls in some detail.

Derrick Kinsley started work as a junior chemist at the steelworks in 1941. He was sent to work in the melting shop and there he met one Bob Harris. He was an older man, and rather ill, suffering from T.B. In 1943, Derrick left to join the navy. After the war, when he returned, he was back in the same workplace, and was told that Bob had died.

The laboratory where Derrick worked was oblong, with a row of benches along one wall, with a sink; on the other side were a hot plate and a fume cupboard. Down the middle there was a long bench for chemicals and bottles. Whoever was working at the hotplate would always have had their back to the person who entered the room.

Derrick was then on a night shift a few months after his return to work, and working at the hotplate when he felt that creepy sensation of being stared at. But he had not heard the door open, and there could be no-one there, logically, at least. But maybe there was no logic in this case? So, he was patient, though stressed and anxious in that atmosphere. He put the feeling down to being over-tired.

But a while later, it all happened again, and this time in an afternoon. This went on repeatedly over a few years. Veiled comments were made by people about 'Bob's ghost.' But then, when Derrick was moved to the Anchor plant, the old melting shop laboratory was pulled down, he was visited by an older man who brought the subject up again. So it became clear that many people had been sure of Bob's presence. He couldn't bear to retire – even in death.

The Twigmoor Hikers

Now this is something from personal experience. It happened on the lonely B road from Kirton to Scunthorpe. In 1980, while driving back from Lincoln with two colleagues from work, it was snowing and stormy. The road was dark as we drove from Greetwell towards the junction at Mortal Ash Hill by Scunthorpe steelworks. My friends were deep in conversation and I was watching the woods at the side of the road. Suddenly, I saw the figure of a man struggling in the wind.

'Stop… there's an old man… he's in trouble,' I said. We all agreed that an old man should not be out in that weather. We pulled up and two of us went back to look for him, only a hundred yards or so behind. There was absolutely no sign of the man. I have since heard that many people have seen the old man there, close to the junction with Holme Lane.

But to add to the mystery of this place, there is also another well-known hiker at almost the same spot. This one is a young woman. A correspondent tells me that this lady flags down drivers and asks for a lift to Kirton. Many have helped her and asked her to take a seat in the back of the car, only to find that, after the vehicle has started up and moved on for a short distance, the hiker has vanished.

Spital Spectre

The village and dairy farm that is now Spital in the Street, fringes the A15 between Lincoln and Brigg. As anyone will know who has driven this stretch, it is one of the most dangerous parts of the long A15 that covers most of the county. As the driver approaches, the red road-sign warns him of the fact that this is a 'red route' and the death statistics are there to remind him of the peril before him. That danger comes from the fact that the road dips suddenly, and several times.

The Romans first made the road and it can provide great beauty, especially when Lincoln Cathedral comes into view as you drive south. But by Spital, there is a long and violent history that is unknown to the average traveller. The early manorial rolls for the county reveal nasty brutality there. In spite of the fact that it was a centre for the Knights Templar and so has a benign past in some ways, beneath the famous history there is the infamous.

Accidents are common; just a year ago, the road was closed after a horrendous crash that left a man dead. The road had to be resurfaced. Could there be something demonic over that stretch of tarmac? There have been sightings of supposed wolves there, even in fairly recent times, but most common of all is the spectre that appears, a face in the mist that appears and swiftly moves closer to the windscreen of the unfortunate driver. Some say that this is the restless spirit of Beatrice Scowt, who was killed in her home in a night attack by a thug called Thomas de Holm.

Whatever the source of this unease on the road, it has happened many times. There have been reports of a figure walking by the road and then turning to face the lights, the face in horror. One account, early last century, is of a woman so emaciated and white that she was at first taken for a skeleton. There is no doubt that on a misty night, a driver on that piece of the road might imagine things, but there is too much substance in the dark lore of the place to remove all belief in the spectre.

HAUNTINGS IN LINCOLN

The city of Lincoln is beautiful, stately and grand. From the Bail in the cathedral quarter the vista across the valley to the Sleaford road and across to Nottinghamshire is magnificent, and the streets around the castle are still medieval in their atmosphere; little has changed in that area, where the walls may keep enclosed the ghosts of the centuries. Close by the castle walls and entrance there are constant reminders of the bloody and warlike history of the Steep Hill and Bailgate alleys and slopes. The regular Friday night ghost walks attract tourists in great numbers, and few are disappointed by the sheer weight of time and human suffering in that place of gaols and scaffolds.

33 Steep Hill

Today this is Browns Pie Shop, and the little place, huddled with other very old premises on the hill, has featured on television in *Derek Acorah's Ghost Towns,* as well as in various local investigations. The most common accounts of paranormal experiences there have been of a child and also of a young girl, but all this is vague. What is far more compelling is a more recent account by Peter Hopper. Peter went there a few years ago, with his family to find information about his great-grandmother. When he arrived it was closed and in darkness, but he wrote in a recent article that an assistant let him go in, and he told the tale of Mary Clayton, his ancestor. In her time the place was The Fox and Hounds, and Peter took a copy of an old photo of the pub before he left. Later, when developed, the picture showed an image of a woman looking through the window. This may or may not be a phantom image. But it does show a shape that is out of proportion with the rest of the material in the composition of the picture.

The Pie Shop has had many inhabitants over the centuries: it was named the Bessy Bedlam at one time, but was the Fox and Hounds back in the late eighteenth century. In other words, there have been people

Brown's Pie Shop.

there in great numbers down the years, and of course, deaths: it may be that the ghosts seen and heard there now are those still in limbo. In that small, enclosed and dark place it is easy to imagine the figures whose spirits lie in shadows, unable to move on to their places of peace. Just to sit in the small front room that is now the café is to feel the events and people of the past centuries pressing into the present.

The television investigators found evidence of a serving boy, the ghost of a child who whispered and touched, as if appealing for help. We have to trust that he was helped to be shifted from that room of pain, but who knows if there are always to be spirits there, grounded and forever loitering in their troubled state. It seems that the ghost of the boy, called by staff Humphrey (as he is so often around that he is almost a member of the team) has been seen by customers as well as by the chef. Certainly the stories go on being told about what looks like a simple tourist café where people take afternoon tea and enjoy their conversation as they sit in the centre of a vestigial history of unsettled spirits.

The Greestone Stairs Phantom

The guide on the official Ghost Walk around Bailgate will tell you with relish about the epicentre of paranormal activity that is Greestone Stairs. Local folk will tell you of a hand that darts out to grasp your ankles as you innocently stroll down the stairs towards the centre of the city. That is the local tale, but far more unsettling are the sighting on the stairs. These range from a young woman to a churchman.

Close to the stairs is a building that used to be a tithe barn and then a hospital. Today it is used by the University of Lincoln, but the fact that it was once a hospital may explain the recurrence of a ghost of a young woman seen on the stairs. She has been seen with a baby in her arms, standing on the stairs, although in most cases her figure is not standing actually on the stone. Accounts of this say that the air is chilled and a feeling of 'time stopped' somehow freezes the time as well as the air. Then the young woman and baby appear, as if the spirit is aching to convey some kind of pain associated with her troubles.

There have also been sightings of a priest on the stairs; people have apparently seen a man in the apparel of a churchman from the Georgian or Stuart period walking up the stairs. He tends to come upwards and then move into a wall. Hearsay would have us believe that there was a suicide there at one time, and certainly that would be a darkly suitable venue for such a horrible event.

But most eerie of all are the hands that are supposed to grab the walker's ankles. That may be hysteria, as the quiet stairs can create an irrational inner fear if the walker is alone, going steadily and carefully down that very steep incline. All I can say is that on one of my own visits there, with a group of other people, a woman sensed that she was held on the arm by something, and that only stopped when she screamed out for help, thinking she was being attacked.

Castle Ghosts

It is hardly surprising that Lincoln Castle should be busy with spirits of past times. There have been frights and battles there over the centuries, and in the grounds there is a dungeon and also the imposing structure of the Victorian prison. Dominating the compound are the Lucy Tower, which is a burial ground for those felons executed in the nineteenth

Cobb Hall Tower.

century, and the Cobb Hall Tower, on which the executions took place up to 1868 when hangings became private.

From folklore we have the most often told tale of the castle: that of the rider who never made it to the place so that he could deliver a pardon for a man sentenced to hang. There have been a few experiences of the horseman dashing to the castle gates and demanding that they be opened; the main story is that the man with the pardon stopped for a drink, had more than one pint, and could not continue; when he finally made it to Lincoln, the condemned man had been hanged.

More recently, there have been investigations in the sombre cells and wings of the old Victorian prison, a miserable building that was used before the new prison on Greetwell Road was opened in 1872. Here, the whole establishment has been preserved for visitors: the matron's room, the cells, the death cell and the turnkey's accommodation. Here, we may grasp the whole process of the prisoner who was to die: the first cells, then the death cell after trial, and a walkway through to a little lane that leads to the hanging tower; and finally his body would be carried up the steep steps to be interred in the Lucy Tower. There is no wonder that ghosts of felons wander the place of their torment.

Investigations by specialist groups in paranormal research have had impressive results from the old prison. One result was evidence of a former inmate called Betsy Potter whose name was heard and then verified by historical research later. There have also been sounds of cell doors shutting and keys being jangled. The problematic orbs of paranormal phenomena have also been seen; these bubbles of whitish matter are not fully understood, but what my records show is that, interestingly, orbs are most prominent when a person has talked about or thought intensely about a loved one who has passed on. There are photographs easily available showing orbs close by people standing at events in which specific relatives who have died are commemorated.

In the prison at the castle, sightings have included a woman in white who walks, staring straight ahead, as if totally fixed on a distant sight or on a thought that sustains her. It is tempting to think that she is one of the two famous people hanged in error at that gaol. In the nineteenth century, there were two notable cases in which after women had hanged, death-bed confessions to the murders were given. Perhaps most celebrated of these is the story of Priscilla Biggadike, who was hanged in 1868 (the first private execution there) and it has later been shown that a man confessed to the murder of her husband.

Today, if you walk into the graveyard in the Lucy Tower, you may see her sunken gravestone, still with the initials visible 'P.B.' in that silent and eerie place. Is it Priscilla who walks in those wings and cells? It may be her, or it may be one of the many other souls who had their necks stretched at Cobb Hall. Under the imposing stone of that tower, above today's car park and gift shops, there have been sightings and sounds of dark and terrible events on the tower top. Just to look up and see the stone sill and castellated stones makes it easy to imagine the scaffold and the swinging corpse, left there for hours to ensure death had taken place. There have been several accounts of sounds of swinging and creaking wood from up there, and other people have heard sighs and moans. Perhaps the most unusual was the account given to me from a man who had heard the sound of cheering and jeering as he walked across the car park. He said it was early one autumn morning, and it came from what is now a restaurant. What he had said fits well with accounts of people buying the best seats at the inns, places from where they could have the best view of the hanging.

Fred Nodder in the Nick

This is the story of a lorry-driver lodger – from Hell. It is disgusting for a crime writer to see the man's name dignified with a place in the reference works of murder now established in reference libraries. But the tale has to be told.

Frederick Nodder moved into new lodgings in Newark in 1935, where his landlady was Mrs Tinsley. He didn't stay long, but he made a mark with the children. To them he was 'Uncle Fred.' He was clearly a man who was difficult to live with, at least in the adult world. When he moved on to East Retford, he still proved to be a handful for the landlady, with his bad habits and tendency to create a mess. Nodder appears to be a man with a mission – to destroy everything and everyone around him that could be classified as weak or vulnerable.

But back in Newark, the large family of Tinsleys was now one short of the usual number. Little Mona, aged ten, was missing. Her father, Wilfred, was frantic with worry. Mona did not return home from her school on the 5 January, 1937. The search began. Her school was not far away and he began his search there. Mona's poor father was distraught with anxiety. After the police were called, the description went out: she was wearing a knitted suit and wore Wellingtons. But a boy called Willie Placket recalled seeing Mona talking to a man and said that he would recognise the man if he saw him again. A Mrs Hird had also seen Mona with a man 'who was a lodger with the girl's mother.' The net was closing in on the person described as 'a man with staring eyes.'

Nodder had a hook nose and his moustache was ginger. Nodder seems to have been memorable, as lots of people remembered him on that journey with little Mona. A bus conductor recalled him. The police traced him to Retford and he was picked up. He had been living as Hudson, and was the father of a child living locally.

Mona had been seen with 'Uncle Fred' and consequently, as Mona was now officially missing and the anxiety increased, Nodder was interviewed. His story was that he had given the girl a lift to Sheffield, and then put Mona on a bus to her aunt's in Worksop. It was all highly suspicious and he was arrested for abduction. There was no body, so there was no murder charge. In court, the abduction still stood and he was sent to prison. As he was in custody and there was a feeling that Mona had been attacked or even killed, a massive search began; 1,000 people joined in to search areas between Retford and Newark. It was such a wide stretch of land that the police from Nottinghamshire, Lincolnshire and Derbyshire all spent time and manpower on the case.

Scotland Yard now sent men to step up the campaign: the Chesterfield Canal was dragged. Nodder had been tried at Birmingham, but now off he went to Nottingham to face a murder charge.

So began Fred Nodder's period inside the walls of Lincoln Prison. Only three months after his trial, Mona's body was found in the River Idle close to Bawtry. Mona had been strangled. Nodder was in court again, trying to tell tales to escape the noose. Nothing he could say did him any good. The presiding judge, Mr Justice Macnaughton, said, 'Justice has slowly, but surely, overtaken you and it only remains for me to pronounce the sentence which the law and justice require...'

The great barrister, Norman Birkett had spoken for the prosecution; it was to be his last trial, appearing for the Crown. It was a terrible case, with a widespread sense of outrage around it, as Nodder had sexually assaulted Mona before killing her. 'Uncle Fred' had turned out to be a monster. The photos of him show a man with a matching flat cap and scarf of small check pattern and a thick overcoat. His eyes are piercing and he shows a face to the world that expresses nothing substantial. 'Something is missing in him' as is often said of these types of killers. Here was a twisted personality who enjoyed inflicting pain on helpless children. It had taken Mona five minutes to die. Ironically, this man who had created so much pain and torment to others lived in a place called 'Peacehaven.'

He was sentenced to hang. A few days after Christmas, 1937, he was in the hands of the hangman and left this world. Or did he? He was hanged in Lincoln Prison on Greetwell Road, and his last moments would have been on the wing of the execution suite. He would have fallen through the trap to dangle and die – very quickly – taking less time to die than his victim had done. The corpse was taken down and buried, with quicklime, as was the custom. But was that the last of Fred Nodder inside the prison walls? Some think not.

Since then, there has been development in the prison, as there has with almost every other Victorian building. Staff report sightings of a man walking the corridors, a man with a dark overcoat and flat check cap. One report is of turning a corner to see a man with piercing eyes coming towards you. Some have merely glimpsed the profile, with the hooked nose and moustache.

There are many dark roads and corners around Greetwell Road. A spirit could wander those streets, a restless, evil entity like Uncle Fred. If the tales are true, then this evil man is as restless now as he was in life – always open to do some horrible mischief. In fairly recent times, when building work was done on the prison site, the graves of executed prisoners were taken up and carried to the city cemetery. The more serious ghost hunters date the appearances of the ghost of Uncle Fred to that time. When the ground opened up, his nasty spirit walked into the world again, out to disturb the unwary. The man with the staring eyes, if he exists in spirit form, will still try his hardest to unsettle the unwary night-walker. Nodder was always a man who haunted, loitered, and watched people.

Even if the Lincoln walker through Greetwell Road has no belief in ghosts, a glance at the forbidding high and dark walls of the prison there will do enough to suggest that this killer had no pleasant stay in his last hours on earth.

Attic Ghost in the Jew's House

A Lincoln man called John de Lexington has a lot to answer for. In 1255, when he was one of a crowd of people who had found the bloated body of a child in a well, he started putting around a story that there was a terrible Jewish custom of indulging in an annual murder of a Gentile child. The body found in the well was that of little Hugh, son of Beatrice, who had been searching the city high and low just a month before, when her son did not return from playing out in the streets.

The mystery at the heart of this story is that Hugh did die, and was found in a cess pool by some of the Jews when they gathered in the home of a man called Jopin to celebrate a marriage. The experience that crowd had is almost too horrendous co contemplate: being together for a happy occasion and then discovering the drowned body of a small boy in their midst. But things turned out sadly wrong for the Jewish community of the city: Jopin, as a result of Lexington's ridiculous urban myth, was tortured to the point at which he confessed to the killing – obviously speaking under extreme duress. But the offer of sparing his life if he confessed was on the table in the rather extreme negotiations.

In Lincoln, in the Dernstall (the Jewish quarter) there had already been a certain degree of discrimination, well before the furore over the supposed murder of Hugh. This was in the early years of the thirteenth century, when a decree issued by the Council of the Church had effected open separatism, by calling the Jews blasphemers and making them dress differently from Christians, and by preventing them furthering their careers by mixing in Gentile society. The paradox at the centre of commercial life in this context, that the local economy needed credit but that usury was sinful, provided just the kind of moral complication that turns men's wits and opens up events to wild prejudice.

As for little Hugh, one advantage of a shrine and a martyr was that more people would visit Lincoln, and that could only be good for trade. But above these practical developments, a myth was engendered about the supposed murder, and this was sustained in literature. A poem of 1783 called *The ballad of Little Sir Hugh* has the lines:

> *'She's led him in through ae dark door,*
> *and sae has she thro nine;*
> *she's laid him on a dressing table*
> *and stickit him like a swine…'*

As time went on, the story was embellished; one account even claims that when the child's body was eventually found by the Christians, 'the hands and feet were pierced with wounds' as if the boy had indeed been crucified. Even Chaucer mentions the event in *The Canterbury Tales*, where he has these lines:

> *'O yonge Hew of Lincoln, slain also*
> *with cursed Jewes, as it is notable,*
> *for it is but a little while ago.'*

A writer much nearer the actual time, Matthew Paris, recounts the events as if it were a matter of fact: '… the Jews of Lincoln stole a boy of eight years of age, whose name was Hugh, and having shut him up in a room quite out of the way… they sent to all the cities of England where Jews lived, and summoned some of their sect who lived in the city to be present at a sacrifice.'

The fate of the other ninety-two Jews was that they were taken to London and tried; Paris reports that 'For on St Clement's Day eighteen of the richer and higher order of the Jews of the city of Lincoln were dragged to new gibbets… and were hung up an offering to the winds.'

What traces are left of this myth are few indeed. There are the remains of a tiny tomb on the north side of the choir aisle in the cathedral. In the eighteenth century, a skeleton was actually found during an excavation, and it was in fact a body of a small child. In the Jew's Court House near the bottom of Steep Hill there is a well which is thought to be the well in question, (though after its discovery by a Mr Harry Staples it was found to be only three feet deep) from the first telling of the tale. The well there, it seems, had been constructed by a Mr Dodgson, much more recently than the time of Hugh. But there is another line of thought, and this traditionally relates that the famous well was where Newport Arch stands.

The Jewish quarter was from Dernstall Lock, at the southern end of the main street, to the southern fringe of Bailgate. The events concerning the taxation imposed on the community after the Hugh affair, and the savagery brought about on the victim Jopin, have to be placed in a context in which there had been very powerful Jewish citizens in Lincoln, and not so long before the death of Hugh. Most notable there is Aaron, who lived in the northern uphill streets somewhere, though not in the house at the top of Steep Hill now called 'Aaron's House' for tourists, opposite the Harlequin bookshop. Aaron was very rich and influential in his time (1166-1186), and the historian Mansell Sympson claims that he was 'possibly the most important financial agent in the kingdom.'

The truth of the supposed murder will never be found; all we know is that, as the famous antiquary Bishop Thomas Percy said, the whole charge is surely 'groundless and malicious, such as been imputed to the Jews for seven hundred and fifty years or more.' The story is as fabricated as the boy's name: he was never canonised, so there is a dark irony in his 'sainthood' as the tale goes on. Even as late as the middle of the

In the nineteenth century, as R. Brimley Johnson notes in an anthology of ballads, as he refers to another ballad on the theme, 'It was known to the labourers of Lincolnshire in very recent years' and in that poem the tale extends to a ghost story, with the spirit of Hugh singing,

> *'Gae hame, gae hame, my mither dear;*
> *Prepare my winding sheet;*
> *And at the back of merry Lincoln*
> *The morn I will you meet.'*

But one thing is for sure: ghostly sights and sounds go on being experienced. There have even been ghosts on photographs, and one of these – an image of a medieval knight – may be the ghost of a certain Solomon of Wallingford who was a coin-clipper back in 1290, and was hanged for his crime.

Theatre Royal Haunted Corner

Theatres and cinemas always seem to have their ghostly guests, and Lincoln Theatre Royal is no exception. The tale that defines the visitation there is one from forty years ago when a member of staff thought he saw someone smoking in a seat near the back of the circle. Of course, what began as a powerful smell of cigar smoke and a sight of a figure seated at the back ended with nothing – except the fact that the seat involved was placed down, as if a person had been there to sit.

That appears to be the pattern in these contexts. The most celebrated example being at Drury Lane, perhaps, where a ghostly presence inhabits a particular seat, and that seat is often found placed down and also heard creaking as someone or something moves it downwards. In Lincoln there is no pattern of that kind, as there are some varieties on the sighting, such as noises heard when the theatre is totally empty; it is clear that a theory of a haunting of public spaces where hundreds of people come together for enjoyment and excitement applies here: a time warp theory in that two contexts of time overlap, like an eclipse. Staircases are often the locus for such crossings, and again, the stairs figure in this, with sounds heard, as if there is movement and activity, then nothing seen.

Yet the line of thought is tempting to pursue – the idea that a certain night of entertainment, with all people involved, was somehow fixed in time, and at some point, people of today sense or see a part of that frozen experience in another time. It is also worth noting that tobacco smoke is a very common example of a sensual comprehension from another time. I have around thirty examples in my casebook of everyday paranormal.

Lesley's Unknown Guest

Lesley's Tea Shop is another place on Steep Hill with a spirit guest, this time most often seen and heard in an attic. The shop is very old, with small rooms and low roofs, as if the physical matter is holding in the presence of former dwellers in the one-time cottage. Staff there tell of an old man, and he is the kind of ghost who resides in a place almost as a member of the family, so familiar is he. One waitress referred to him as Fred, but whether all agree on that name is not certain.

Tom tends to appear by surprise. Someone will open a door and there he is. It appears that he wants to make staff jump, as a twisted joke. But that is the only slightly unlikeable thing about him: it would be going too far to call his presence malevolent in any way.

On one occasion, someone carrying a tray felt that she was being gently pushed, as might happen if one were being teased. At other times he has been heard, a mumbled few words said from an empty room. Everything points to the ghost being a man who lived there for a long time, and now is truly rooted to the place he called home. Staff have to just accept that there is one more inhabitant and that he might appear at any time. His most recent appearance was on Halloween 2008 when the phone rang and was answered by someone before staff came.

Tom Otter

Local ghost-hunting groups, most recently the researchers from Bassetlaw, have spent nights on the premises of the Sun Inn, at Saxilby, just outside Lincoln, close to Doddington Hall. This is because some reckon that this particular pub is the most haunted one in England. The reason for this is that it has a link to one of the most brutal and callous murders ever committed in Lincolnshire: the killing of his new wife by Tom Otter, otherwise known as Thomas Temporel. Like so many aspects of the Otter story, we are not sure where the truth lies.

But what we can be certain about are the facts of the murder, although the details about the key witness to this are troublesome. The witness was John Dunkerly, a labourer from north of Drinsey Nook towards the village of Harby, who had enjoyed a night at the Sun in November, 1805. Talk must have been full of the battle of Trafalgar, only two weeks before this, and other topics related to Napoleon and Nelson. It was a long night, and Dunkerly had to walk home, several miles through dark, lonely moorland.

Earlier accounts of Dunkerly, based on a long statement he made in court, suggest that he was a 'peeping Tom' who had a habit of walking out to lonely spots in search of courting couples. But he may have been simply tired, stopping at a field corner, and falling asleep. Whatever the facts of the actual circumstances, he saw Tom Otter and his wife, Mary Kirkham, together, and he reported that Otter had sat her down, said, 'Sit down, you can rest here.' Then he walked into the undergrowth and grabbed a hedge-stake. This was on 3 November, the day he had married Mary at South Hykeham; she was pregnant by him and, of course, he was forced to marry, under pressure. But now, in the darkness, thinking they were alone, he said, 'This will finish my knob-stick wedding' ('shotgun wedding' in modern terms). It certainly did. Dunkerley saw everything.

Dunkerly was a casual labourer, and on that day he had taken some time off, sitting in the Sun, and at that time, the pub would have been open from half past five in the morning through until midnight. Dunkerly left his friends around six o'clock and started the long walk. His statement notes that he passed two men he knew near Drinsey Nook, and that they said, 'You'll have company, John.' They referred to the newly-weds, and this may have given rise to the image of Dunkerly as a man who scouted around for titillating vicarious pleasure in his voyeurism.

If he was in a thick hedge, then Otter came very close to him as he chose the hedge stake. Then, as Dunkerly describes, he noted that comedy, not tragedy, began:

'The moon shined on his face at the time and his eyes frightened me, there was such a fiery look in them…Then he climbed down to where she was sitting with her head hanging down, and he swung the hedge stake with both hands and hit her a clout on the head. She gave one scream and called on God for mercy, then tumbled over with her head on the ground.'

Dunkerly's account is convincing and graphic in its details; he even noted that Mary's body was 'all a-quiver like' before she became rigid. He described the second blow as being like hitting a turnip. With remarkable self-control, Dunkerly kept his silence. But it seems as though he passed out. When he awoke, the stake was near him, and there was some of Mary's blood on the sleeve of his smock.

The witness panicked at this and took to wandering around the area for a while, not knowing what to do. But the body was found and Otter was arrested. He was found at the Sun Inn, and also the inquest was held there, the body being taken to the inn after being found. Here begins the kind of detail that led to the tale of Tom Otter being a standard Lincolnshire ghost story: blood dripped from Mary's body onto the steps of the Sun. The hedge stake was kept at the inn, as a piece of customer interest and good local 'spin' for attracting travellers with an interest in gruesome stories.

Otter's trial lasted for five hours, with Justice Graham presiding. It cannot have been worse than the inquest, where poor Mary's corpse had been laid out for all to see, with the gore-stained hedge stake nearby. Not only was Otter sentenced to hang, but also it was ordered that his body be gibbeted. This was the practice of hanging the corpse of a murderer high above a road for all the birds to peck and consume, as a warning to others to keep to the law. A gibbet was a high post with an arm out, from which either the entire corpse or a limb would be placed. By the end of the eighteenth century, this was becoming a rare practice; but in the Otter case, his deed was so reprehensible that some horrible symbolic token of justice was needed. Otter was hanged in March, 1806 and the irons and gibbet for him were made by a Saxilby man, the blacksmith, Dick Naylor. Otter was 'stretched' on Cobb Hall tower at the corner of the castle; the great bell, known as Great Tom, struck twelve.

Then the legends began. When the gibbet was raised into position, the weather was severe and there was a strong wind. After all, it was 30 feet high, and was raised by block and tackle. As an earlier writer, Thomas Burke, noted in 1933: 'Nature seemed to be on the side of the murderer.' This was because the beam broke twice, and at one point the metal tackle fell down on the labourers. When it was all done, the story is that Dunkerly said, 'Well, he won't come down no more.' Then Tom Otter's remains fell down on him.

The saga of the hedge stake is at the heart of the legend. It was supposed to go missing on November 4 every year; after being fixed to the wall, this still happened on the next anniversary. Finally, the Sun landlord sent it to the Peewit Inn not far away. A blacksmith used six clamps to fix this to a wall, but it went missing again. The end of this fantastic tale is that the stake was ceremonially burned by the walls of Lincoln Cathedral, the burning done by order of the Bishop himself.

John Dunkerly, whether we want to believe him or not, had undergone far more trauma as a result of his witnessing the murder than anyone knew until, as he lay dying, he told a tale of a terrible haunting to the minister who came to his bed-side, including appearances by the ghost of Tom Otter himself. Dunkerly explained that the worst torments were on the anniversary nights of the murder:

' ... I felt doley-like so I went to bed about dusk-hours, and what I'm trying to tell you is as true as that I'm a dying man. I couldn't nohow sleep and all of a sudden Tom Otter stood in front of me in his chains, and he says, "It's time. Come along." And I had to go with him. And he says, "Fetch it. Make haste." And I broke into the Sun inn and fetched the hedge stake from off the nail... when I got outside the door, they were both waiting for me.'

The gibbet stayed there until around 1850. Parts of this terrible object may still be seen by visitors to Doddington Hall. But the myth goes on: the judge, Basil Neild, writes in his memoirs about the case, and he recalls a rhyme written as a riddle, composed by an anonymous local poet:

> '10 tongues in one head
> 9 living and one dead.
> One flew forth to fetch some bread
> To feed the living in the dead.'

The answer? Of course, it's 'The tomtit that built in Tommy Otter's head.'

The myth of Tom Otter/Temporel will go on and on, as it has all the elements of a folk tale, enough to keep people awake by the fireside when they are in the mood for a ghost story. Even today, at the Sun Inn, it is hard to avoid the sense of this dark and brooding past in that wild place that it was when Tom was there.

In Saxilby today, there is still much to see and to imagine in relation to the terrible tale of Tom Otter and his new wife.

The Presence in the Cellar

One of the most well-known shops in Lincoln is on the corner where Steep Hill winds slightly down into its second stage, opposite the Harlequin bookshop. This is a very old building, having a plaque on the wall informing visitors that it was Aaron the Jew's house in the medieval period. Today, its cellar is accessible at the lower level from the street, as the street slopes downwards. Outside is a bench where climbers may pause and rest on the way up the hill. Little do those walkers know that behind them, in the cellar, is a focal point of ghostly activity.

Investigation teams have been, and a few years ago, television medium Derek Acorah was there. It was positively vibrant with life from some other dimension. At that time is was a gift shop and is now a tea and coffee retail area, and it may be that something in the refurbishment has changed things; but there used to be a malevolent presence down there, something that would have been called a sprite in Shakespeare's world. It would be going too far to call this spirit a poltergeist, as its activities were usually more confined to pressing against legs and arms,

Medieval cellar entrance.

and also moving items across the room. The television investigation found it to be malicious and most likely a spirit of a suicide.

This ghost is grounded, and is always there, with quiescent periods and then a burst of activity. There appears to have been a whispering and a moaning sound when Acorah was there. But as with all manifestations in busy, tourist-frequented places, it is hard to have access there at a quiet time, of course.

The White Hart Ghost Room

Hotel staff do not like it known that one of their rooms is haunted. In the case of the White Hart Hotel in Bailgate, it may be admitted that there is a 'bad' room, but everyone is sworn to secrecy when it comes to giving the room number to strangers and researchers. But, regardless of exactly where these things happen, the evidence is clear: a young man who took his own life is the most likely candidate for the identity of the ghost within the walls of the hotel, although there is another connection with an accident more than a century ago.

There have been gunshots heard and bright lights seen, and also a ghost of what seems to be a highwayman, but the real focus here is on the room in question. I have been told that there is nothing there to cause an alarm, but that at times there is a sense of sadness and it is localised. One of the outstanding features of the human sensitivity to the presence of an unhappy spirit is a spontaneous weeping, and a feeling of some sadness being shared; this appears to be the complex human capacity for expressing compassion in terms of our empathic ability.

The White Hart Inn.

In cases of suicide, such as this may be, that empathy, an ability mediums possess, expresses itself in the sensitivity to sound and movement emanating from something unexplained. It may simply be a movement like a shadow or that alleged gunshot from many years ago.

The other possibility for a ghost – this time outside the hotel, and sometimes at the entrance – is of a man who has been seen with a horse-whip and wearing boots and coat as if he is travelling or about to leave. This is possibly the ghost of a man called William Glasier, from Aply, who died when his gig turned over; this happened just after he left the hotel. Such hauntings are quite common, as the location of a beginning of a journey or the end of a journey appears to be a point of paranormal activity, a focal location in which a fateful experience is trapped in timelessness, seen or heard by those with a perception of the dead. The White Hart does seem to gather more than its fair share of reportings of the paranormal: there have been supposed ghostly children playing, a figure of a Victorian woman, and a soldier who appears to want help from the living with quite trivial sounding matters, though to that spirit they may be vitally important.

The Jolly Brewer Visitors

The Jolly Brewer sits prominently on a corner on the main road through the centre of Lincoln out towards the south, Broadgate. It is opposite the old Drill Hall and close to car parks, so customers and travellers always notice it. But there is a ghostly presence that appears to want the attention of the staff, not simply to acknowledge the pub as an interesting and welcome sight. This is a ghostly voice, rather than a sighting of anything inexplicable.

This phantom voice calls out on the staff, wanting their attention, and does not have any interest in attracting the attention of customers. There is no more detail given about this worrying call from beyond; the voice is ostensibly without a perceivable body; but the landlady has said that she has heard it call her name, and so have many members of staff.

The other tale sometimes told about the pub is the ghost of a young man who had his stag night there in the 1970s and who later died in a road crash not far away. There have been tales of him singing and talking about his car and how it was mangled in the crash; he has been known to loiter outside and in the entrance and catches hold of a person's sleeve or coat to tell the woeful story of his death and yet to say he loves the Brewer. He has talked about his friend, a man called Colin, who survived the crash.

Clark's Dog

In 1877, a fearsome character called William Clarke went out poaching with two mates. Two of them carried guns, and in a place called Eagle Wood they met Henry Walker, a gamekeeper. When Clarke and friends were told to stop, the poachers ran away but were followed. As the pursuit developed, Clarke turned and shot Walker twice, in the knee and thigh. It took the gamekeeper a long time to die; he was in agony for days, as doctors amputated a limb in an attempt to save him.

Clark went on the run across the county and police were after him, in all areas. Superintendent Brown of Kesteven went after the killer and finally cornered him in Lowestoft at the White Horse. Clark was taken for trial in Lincoln and there, his accomplice, Garner, turned Queen's evidence and Clark was identified as the man who fired the gun. He was hanged by William Marwood.

Clark had a faithful dog, a Skinny Lurcher, and as with all his acquaintance, the poor animal received beatings most weeks. Clark was supposed to like the bar at the Strugglers Inn and there the dog would be with him, expecting either a clout or sometimes a stroke. After his master's arrest, the dog had no home of course. It was supposed to have hung around the pub for a while, feeding on scraps of food. When the next hanging came along, the dog would howl in a most horrific way and so the usual dramatic events of the hanging were even more exciting for the gathering crowd.

But the dog's spirit goes on, and to this day, it's said that around the castle at times can be heard the horrible yelping of Clark's dog. People say they have seen him in the shadows and heard his whining, as the poor desperate animal's spirit goes on in torment, as indeed it was in life with its brutal master, a man who ended swinging on a rope.

GHOSTS ACROSS
THE COUNTY

Black Dog Ghosts

Stories of ghostly dogs are legion across Britain. They all have different local names, from the black shuck of East Anglia to the Gytrash of Yorkshire. In Lincolnshire, most experiences of seeing and hearing these spectral dogs have been in clusters around Brigg, on the Trent, and in the Fens. There is a particularly rich area where there have been a number of sightings – in Laughton Forest north of Gainsborough. The origins of black shuck lie somewhere between medieval folklore and the testimony of witnesses who have spoken to historians and paranormal investigators. It has never been clear exactly what the black shuck is, as interpretations vary.

It is best to begin with an actual story. An ex-police officer, a man very fond of his Alsatians, went for a morning walk with his dogs in Laughton Forest. He reported that after playing for a while, the two dogs froze and stared towards a specific spot in the undergrowth. They would not go any nearer to the vegetation and began to growl. This was totally out of character, the man said as he was interviewed. He went closer, and he talked about seeing a pair of eyes in the undergrowth and then something moved. He saw the dimensions and said that they were the size of a horse, not a dog. He ran from the spot, back into his car, where the dogs were already sitting, in fear. He drove off. 'It couldn't have been a puma or any kind of big cat' he said, 'I saw the outline of its back. It was like a racehorse.'

As far back as 1577, in Bungay, Suffolk, there have been accounts of these black dogs entering churches and homes, and creating havoc. One researcher, Theo Brown, has written that there were 39 incidents involving black shuck between 1829 and 1958 – incidents that were hard to explain away by rational means. Some of the earlier accounts talk of a shape-shifting dog – and that sort of dimension adds credence to the folklorist approach to understanding the phenomenon. But there are two notable experiences in fairly recent times that add to the belief that Lincolnshire seems to be a focus for these apparitions.

The first was recalled by a tramp who had been walking from Caenby to Stow. He said that as he walked at dusk not far from Glentham where there is a sharp dip as the escarpment falls towards the North Nottingham plain, he was aware of a 'companion.' He sensed from the corner of his eye that it was taller than he, but that there was a smell, as if some cloth or skin was burning. Finally, he dared to look sideways and he expected to see a fellow hobo. But it was a black dog, 'the size of a small horse, its eyes yellow and its breath stinky like candle smell, like tallow…' He didn't know whether to sit, try to hide or run for it. But as he thought about his options, it walked sideways away from him and vanished.

Then there was the soldier in the forties, home from the war and unable to find a lift to Brigg. He reported seeing a huge dog, and in the afternoon in summer, by Twigmoor woods. He swore that he had no whisky on him and had not taken a drop, but described the apparition as 'somehow not threatening… like some freak of nature but not interested in me.' It walked off in another direction as he was cowering in the bushes, praying.

Writing in 1951, Alasdair MacGregor gathered some black dog stories, some from the famous Lincolnshire folklorist, Ethel Rudkin of Willoughton. One story he had was from Kesteven, in Haconby: a brother and sister, walking near their home in the 1930s, used to take a short-cut in the dark, and walk through Bourne Wood. On more than one occasion the black dog would come to walk by them. It walked as far as a hand-gate.

Even more documented is the presence of the black dog in the Isle of Axholme, notably around Gunthorpe, and Ethel Rudkin had a memory from a man there; he said he had seen the black dog in Intake Lane, and that his friend Sammy Prettle had once tried to shoot it. The man said, ' Sammy once shot at it by a big willow tree… and his gun-barrel busted, and he came home white as a sheet.'

Arguably the most haunted spot for black dog appearances in the county is Belle Hole near Kirton in Lindsey. At a meeting of local historians in 1936 it was discussed, and a local school mistress talked about seeing the dog, saying, '…I often see him while cycling back to Manton alone, after a lecture or a whist-drive at Kirton.' At Belle Hole during the same period, locals claimed that they knew where the black dog lived.

MacGregor wrote:

'That the country people believe implicitly in the existence of the Black Dog at Belle Hole is shown by the readiness with which they identify, in the bank of a stream there, the hole in which they say he lives…... In 1935 a farmer's wife at Belle Hole actually saw the Black Dog enter the farmhouse kitchen, where she happened to be at the time. She watched him as he walked round it and then left as he had entered. She remained perfectly still throughout the duration of his visit…'

Experiences with the black dog around Grayingham, Kirton and Willoughton seem to have been frequent occurrences in the early and middle years of the last century. One woman in Grayingham said that she met the dog once and tried to strike it with her umbrella. She said that 'the umbrella went clean thruff 'im.'

What is to be made of these sightings? Maybe they lie somewhere between hallucinatory visions and distortions of something else. Most rational arguments say that they are more likely to be pumas, but seen from unusual angles. Whatever perspective we take, the result is that the sightings go on, and many have features in common. Lincolnshire appears to be one of the places they move about in, and enjoy appearing to people. The search for the truth about shuck goes on.

Murder Field, Kirton

There is a field corner near Grayingham, and it looks as bland as any other everyday view of nature, seen from the car as people speed towards Lincoln or Kirton. But this is the corner of a murder place, a killing that happened back in 1847. In a feature for a local paper back in 1954, the journalist 'Wayfarer' summed up the local feeling about it: ' this is a gate near which no grass will grow.'

The feature reports that, 'It is a fascinating yarn that Kirton folk still tell to their children and grandchildren. For the story springs from the town's most notorious murder.' There are many features in the actual narrative that help us to understand why there should be a myth around this. What is essentially a tale of two drunken friends falling out leads to much more, and the events tell us a great deal about the nature of murder investigations at the time.

A few days before Christmas, 1847, Joseph Travis and his friend

Charles Copeman went for a drink or two and they were seen arguing. On the Sunday morning afterwards, Copeman was found dead in the field, in a ditch with his head severely bruised, his throat cut and, as the first report stated, 'quite dead.' There had been a very vicious attack, of such extent that even the man's dog was found with him, stabbed and bruised. *The Lincoln, Rutland and Stamford Mercury* on Christmas Eve, delivered a detailed account of the discovery of the body:

> *"On Sunday morning at about nine o'clock, as John Whelpton, a labouring man, was proceeding to Kirton along the bridle path leading from Grayingham, his attention was attracted by a dog sitting on something by the road-side which... he discovered to be a human body with the face downwards and the dog sitting upon the back. ... Two other men came up directly but none of them dare approach.'*

Whelpton did some elementary observation as a constable was called by another man, and he noted that there were footmarks discernible matching the dead man's boots from the Kirton direction, and another set of footprints from the east side, joining the victim's. Not far from the body there were obvious signs of a desperate struggle, and also a wallet with two half crowns, a shilling and a six-pence piece.

When the law arrived and a crowd had gathered, the body was moved and there was the face of the man all bystanders would have known. There was a deep wound on the left of his face; a slash had cut across and down across the jugular. There was a cut below one eye and another down the side of the whole face to one side. The nasal bone was broken. The attack had been savage and brutal: there was a severed ear and a gash from the ear to the throat. The conclusion was that, as there was no blood on the man's breast, the wounds had been inflicted when the victim was down on his back.

It was assumed that there had been more than one assailant and several men were arrested and questioned in Gainsborough, about ten miles away, on Monday. A handbill was circulated with a reward of £100 for the apprehension of the killer. The local suspects were arrested simply on hearsay concerning their presence that night, or because of their known characters. Joseph Travis, however, emerged as the main suspect, albeit on circumstantial evidence. Travis was twenty-four, a joiner and cabinet make, the son of a local farmer. *The Lincolnshire Chronicle* reported on 31 December that Travis was 'respectably connected' but that he had 'for some time led a most dissipated life and has lost considerable sums

at card playing.' When questioned, Travis, according to one contemporary reporter, 'gave a statement replete with gross contradictions.'

Travis did not hang, but was sentenced to transportation. One story
says that he tried to jump overboard and was shot. Whatever the truth,
the field corner and gate have a certain sombre atmosphere today, and
'Wayfarer' wrote that ' A legend grew up that no grass would ever grow
on the spot where the murder took place…'

What can be noted is that two or three walkers in the area have
commented on the charged atmosphere of that little stretch of land and
the gate. It's strange that nobody wants to linger there, even though it is
beautiful country, more know for its stables and peacefulness than for its
restless spirits.

Gainsborough Angel

Sorting through the historical papers in a small publication of some
decades ago, the strangest paranormal story surely ever told of
Gainsborough was related, and it was a story confirmed at the time as
true by two ministers of the church and three honest, respectable gentlemen of the town. It all happened on 4 April, 1819 and events began with
the church bells tolling most sweetly. That would have been most
welcome, except that John Coulston, who was clerk, and the sexton, had
the keys. There was a locked church, with nobody inside, but a wonderful peal of bells.

Mr King, the clergyman, was due to preach that day, and the two
men went to fetch him. As the three men entered the church, King said a
prayer: he was seemingly expecting something inexplicable (rather than
a mere prankster). 'Our Heavenly Father, we surrender ourselves at Thy
call' he said as they went in, fearfully, to see what was happening.

They reached the belfry and there they looked around, and after a
few seconds they saw a child, 'clothed in white, with a crown of gold on
his head and who by means alone of the breath of his mouth, put the bells
in motion, and made them ring harmoniously…' King asked the child
who he was, and the response was that he was the messenger of the Lord,
'I am come to exhort all men to repentance.'

The angel's words seem close to that of a street-corner preacher, as
he talked about preparing them 'for the terrible day of the last judgement
when the world shall be destroyed by fire.' It was a hell and brimstone

sermon from the child. He said that the Lord would 'torment the Christian nations in his anger.' King spoke again to the angel, ' How knowest thou these things?'

'My Heavenly master does not deliver them to his servants, but he has sent me…'

The most stunning experience was to follow. The angel led the men to the interior and told them to lift a stone. None of the men could lift it, but the angel-child did so very easily, and he took a scroll of paper from underneath. He read the words, 'England… renounce thy wickedness and hasten to repentance.'

The angel disappeared, the men said, to the sound of melodious music. The witnesses to this bizarre experience wrote their names and dated the vision: on 4th April, 1819 they saw this – 'Mr King and Mr Horn, Ministers; Mr Chambers, John Coulston and John Boon, gentlemen.'

Epworth Rectory Again

We return now to Epworth Rectory, home of the Wesleys, and to more tales of their suffering at the mercy of their evil spirit.

Further disturbances with the Wesley family poltergeist involved Charles's wife, Susanna. The poor woman tried to keep the awful torments of 'Old Jeffrey' from everyone. Susanna saw that the youngest children in her brood were frightened and could not sleep. But, although the father of the house was not troubled by the restless spirit, the time came for Susanna to tell him what had been going on.

The rector himself was then disturbed, as he awoke to find that a knocking was rousing him in fear; so much was he worried that he loaded his pistol, and after that he became more of a victim, with his own possessions being thrown around. Jeffrey went into a very noisy phase and hurled kitchen utensils across the room and made any small object within reach jump up and down. The family noted that they had all had a similar feeling of being shoved out of a room and along into another one.

There was no doubt then that there had to be an exorcism. This was the Rev. Mr Hoole, and he joined with Charles to do battle with the demonic sprite in the home. They both dressed for the struggle, wearing black and powdering their wigs; they went into the nursery, as that was where Jeffrey spent most time causing mischief. Apparently, one bed went up into thin air and Mr Hoole had to consider plan B. He began the ritual, and spoke the usual words, bidding the poltergeist be gone; there was a certain level of success in this, because activities gradually decreased and stopped, but this was not an immediate achievement at all.

There have been accounts of all this which blame the daughter Hetty for all of this, but the writer and folklorist Andrew Lang wrote in the journal of the Society for Psychical Research that it is likely that young Mary Wesley was perhaps the unknowing channel of communication through which a real poltergeist acted. The haunting at Epworth went on for so long and was so well documented, that it carries an extraordinary degree of substance and demands attention from researchers.

Two Grantham Ghosts

This is a hotel with a massive paranormal reputation, and deservedly so. It has been there for many centuries, going back to the reign of King John, and he stayed there in 1217. Its full name is the Angel and Royal Hotel, and its most persistent resident ghost is that of the White Lady. Grantham has its fair share of ghosts, including the poltergeist in the Blue Pig pub and the museum ghost, but the White Lady is a stunning subject – the sightings have been frequent and convincing. In 2001 an American staying there came to breakfast and asked staff why they had not told her the place was haunted? She had been woken up by the White Lady at the foot of her bed. The apparition had stood there for a while and then walked away.

The descriptions keep coming and they tally: the spectral woman is slim, average height, has her hair in a plait and always has the long white dress with the fitted bodice. Unfortunately there is no verified story of the woman she was when alive and on earth. But she is rooted there. The manager a few years ago was Tony Chang, and he reported seeing her as he was tidying up when dinner was coming to an end; the ghost walked across to the place in the wall where there was formerly a staircase.

As the hotel began as a home of the famous Knights Templar, there is no surprise that it has a spiritual dimension, in many senses. But in contrast, King's School seems to be just as active, though a secular establishment. There is no sure knowledge about who the ghost of King's

School was, but he is there for sure.

The most convincing sighting was when the old boys of the school met in a pub and started talking about their experiences. One said, ' He is dressed in black – real old fashioned clothes' and another: ' He's got a great cape on with baggy sleeves and a floppy white tie.' The ghost usually walks swiftly by, in a straight line, fixed on a particular destination. He is reputed to walk through the school and then out into Castlegate. When called, he does not respond. One ex-student said that he tried that once: 'Doesn't pay you any attention… I called out to him and he never turned around…' Could it be the ghost of the great Isaac Newton? Some of the old boys might think so, but writer Rupert Matthews says, ' He would have been dressed in a hard-wearing woollen suit of a farmer's son, not the silk cloak and cravat of the gentleman he was to become…'

Dog at the Gate, Scampton

The great 'Dambusters' left for their momentous flight into Germany from RAF Scampton in 1943, a few miles north of Lincoln. Until a few years ago, a Wellington bomber stood at the front gates of that airfield, but now, the most interesting sight you might see there will be the ghost of Nigger, Guy Gibson's Labrador.

Nigger is seen fairly regularly, both around the gates and elsewhere. In fact, he has reputedly been seen at Woodhall Spa as well. One memory is of seeing him on a photo: ' A photograph of a group or airmen revealed a black dog standing at the end of the line up that was not spotted at the time by either the photographer or any of the pilots. It was later suggested that it was Nigger… who had been run over a few months before.' It has also been pointed out that at the end of the film, *The Dam Busters*, when Wallace is talking to Gibson, a black Labrador is seen running through the trees, and no dog was on site at the time.

All this may seem questionable, and part of a general will to believe in such a wonderful tale about a heroic figure such as Gibson, but now enter the investigation group, Believe Team. This intrepid paranormal investigation outfit went to Scampton and this is what they reported:

'So through the night we split into groups so we could cover each area… Seki Turned around and said, 'What the hell is that?' Nick then turned and both of them could see this black dog in the distance… They

then started walking towards the dog and both of them definitely said it was a black Labrador, the same breed as Guy Gibson's dog which is seen on a regular basis…'

The dog ran away and the camera was too late to grab a shot of the animal. Was it simply a stray dog? We will never know. All we do know is that sightings of the dog who may be Nigger have been frequent, and have carried on for many years.

Hemswell and East Kirkby RAF Stories

Keen enthusiasts of the paranormal will recall the *Most Haunted* investigation at East Kirkby. The two highlights of that programme were undoubtedly the tale of the hapless pilot who was told he could not land, and then when he did so, he crashed and died, and the noises and shadows on camera of a ghost who was clearly moving about in one of the hangars. East Kirkby is clearly not only haunted but infiltrated by spirits who died violently in that terrible time of the fighter wars over Britain.

The base is where the Aviation Heritage Centre is now located; there visitors may see a Lancaster bomber and a control tower. The latter is where one of the ghosts of the base is reported to be. The figure seen is of an American flyer, in his uniform, and he tends to walk close to the tower and pulls behind him a burning parachute. The general feeling is that he may have been on the crew of The Belle of Liberty, the one that was not given permission to land and made an emergency landing. Derek Acorah, on the television investigation at East Kirkby, picked up on this and gave interesting and convincing information about the young airman and his sad death. There have been other figures seen walking to the tower as well.

Mediums tend to pick up the emotions of rage, injustice and vengeance, or on some effort to communicate feelings about a wrongful act. That certainly made sense at East Kirkby when Acorah applied his talents to the case.

Hemswell, once a set of ruins, is now an antique centre. Its collection of World War II airplanes, once on display, has now gone. There is a prosperous feel to the place, but little to evoke the RAF of former times.

The base has been remarkable for a range of auditory phenomena,

Tower at RAF Hemswell.

though there have also been visible experiences. The most notable are arguably the ghostly sounds of engines, men shouting commands and greetings, and also noise of trucks and jeeps on the move, heard occasionally on the air base when it was operational. There have been stories of other presences there also, such as a spirit that sometimes presses and pushes on people as they walk in particular areas. There has to be a certain level of expectation of dramatic and stressful scenes in such a place, of course, and so the kind of image seen at East Kirkby is likely to be seen in any base, and that applies at Hemswell too, though sightings have been infrequent.

Ghosts in the Garden

In what other place would you least expect a paranormal experience than in the garden? That blessed plot where we expect peace and solace is hardly meant to be a location for ghostly activity, yet the appeals for stories for this collection has brought in some remarkable disturbances from the other world, among flower beds and vegetable plots. One correspondent wrote:

'It was early spring and I was resting in the sitting room, looking out at the fruit bushes not much beyond sticks and planning to go and do some digging in of the good stuff I'd built up on the compost... when I saw this figure... it was my grandfather, to a tee, wearing just the old green jacket he did, and the corduroy trousers. I could tell by the movements that it was him... I ran outside to shout, my heart thumping in my throat. I mean, I had no idea what I was going to say... but when I got out there, course, he was gone.'

The supposed tranquillity of the garden is for some entirely wrong; a correspondent from Caistor described to me a chilling account of 'something not of this world' which used to appear quite regularly outside his greenhouse. While he was working quietly, he would sense that he was being watched. When it first happened, he looked towards the grimy windows by his side and felt sure that he could make out a pair of eyes watching him. He ran out to see if his wife was calling him in for tea, as she sometimes came out and tapped on the window.

'I admit that the glass in most of my greenhouse was mucky, ' he said, 'But one time when I looked up, I could see a sort of face – like it was blurred, and it seemed to ripple as if light was passing over it...'

He would have long periods when nothing at all happened, and then one day there it would be again. He checked all sides in case there was an intruder, but the garden is very private and enclosed. Then it stopped happening. But there is one coda to the story. He used to keep a torch on the wall outside for extra light when it was dusk. On one occasion, this torch was thrown at the glass. He distinctly heard a smash and ran out, ready for trouble. The torch had hit the glass, but there was no damage done – not so much as a scratch.

The torch was on the ground, and there was a mark across it, as if it has been placed on something hot and had been slightly burned.

Grimsby Ghosts

Of the most compelling stories of ghostly presences in Grimsby, the case of the Yarborough Hotel has to take prominence. It has been in the town since 1851, when it was owned by the second earl, and was handy for the new railway. Although the pub was the scene of brawls and riots in the election ferment of the 1870s and 1880s, it is hard to link its most frequently seen ghost to anything from those events.

This is because the spirits resident there appear to be children, sometimes heard in the cellar. There have been reports of the sound of children playing and laughing, apparently from several members of staff. It has been hard to trace any historical source for this, but one theory might be the history of unrest there that did involve all members of families, back in the days when riots became a free for all and the establishment took both flak and abuse from all ages.

Any disturbance in the hotel may be related to the 1862 riot – something so extreme that much of the interior was wrecked; the police had been standing by all day, amid fears about trouble after two strangers came into town to organise a campaign. That was always a sign of real street violence if not controlled. The Yarborough has been the epicentre of such street violence on several occasions, and that restlessness has maybe carried into the fabric of the place.

More startling is the appearance of a most alarming ghost at Nun's Corner, a place most associated by locals with the college; but at his house there, Robin Furman reported seeing a ghostly nun; he recalls that 'I reached the top of the stairs and there she was, a tall nun. I could see her quite clearly and she looked completely real.' The only unusual aspect was the fact that instead of a head, the figure had a light, a 'glowing light' Robin stated. He could see that her head-dress and wimple were those of days long gone, so there was immediate proof that this was no nun of today. He then said that she 'drifted away and was gone. It all happened so quickly that I didn't have time to be scared.'

Boston Hauntings

Boston Stump, otherwise known at St Botolph's church, in the scene of a famous legend: the notoriously windy nature of the very top is ascribed to the fact that the original monk, Botolph himself, used to pray up there with such vigour that he disturbed the devil himself, and so the winds around there are caused by Old Nick.

But a more directly unnerving and melancholy tale associated with the Stump is a suicide – or so it seems to be. There have been sightings of a young woman who appears to leap from the tower, speed downwards to her doom, but then vanish into thin air. Of course, this is a common pattern where a site of a suicide is documented. There are various possibilities in this case, from places quite near, but no record of a suicide of a young woman who threw herself from the tower; but there may be some candidates from other research.

Roadside Hauntings

Lincolnshire is particularly rich in paranormal happenings on its roads. Of course, being largely rural, with plenty of tracks and B roads, the county has all the geographical features that would make sightings at dusk or early morning always subject to tricks of light. But it is remarkable how many truly bizarre sightings have been made in this context. Arguably the most terrifying is what many claim to be a vampiric figure on the motorway between Scunthorpe and Elsham top, about half a mile from the junction leading to the road over to the Humber Bridge. There have been at least three reports of this, usually happening in the early hours of the morning. The M180 is obviously very quiet then, and it seems to be that a blurred and amber-coloured shape manifests by the road and then is localised about a hundred yards in front of the moving car. For a second or two a figure looking like a vampire closes on the window, and then disappears.

There is also a sprinkling of ghosts at places where there recorded road deaths, notably on the B1431, the Laceby to Louth road. Some years ago a lorry driver was on the road, his load being concrete, and he was driving in pouring rain as he came to a bend a little way past the junction with the North Thoresby road. The man reported that he saw in front of him a figure on horseback, wearing black, with his back to the lorry; the driver reported that, naturally, his response was that it made no sense at all. If it was a present-day rider, he clearly would not be on that road at such a time. But what he saw next was the man being thrown from the horse.

What the driver then did next confirms the nature of one of the most standard, sheer template stories of ghosts: a violent death. This is because, as the driver looked around in astonishment, he saw a gravestone – something that turned out to be a memorial stone, though shaped like a cemetery stone. Jared Williams first investigated this, and he saw the stone, with this inscription: 'This stone marks the spot where George Nelson of Cadeby Hall was killed, January 16th 1885, aged 16 years.'

The lorry driver told his tale to a colleague, and that man had experienced exactly the same vision on the road. The historical records confirmed the brief account given on the memorial stone.

Jared Williams also collected other road apparitions, notably a story he was told by a woman who related this tale after he gave a talk. She said that she was driving to Grimsby at dawn and as she came close to Wraithe she saw in front of her a horse-drawn cab. She was concerned because the vehicle had no lights on, and that was dangerous, of course; but she passed the cab, aiming to help, when she glanced behind her, and there was no cab to be seen anywhere. She checked that there was no junction at which the cab, if real, could have turned off the road.

Finally, in Jared's collection, we have the story of the burning house by the side of the A16 close to Louth. A couple were driving and saw the fire, so went to investigate. They turned off and saw a fire in full power, with firemen present and a woman shouting from an upstairs window. They drove on, but the next day they contacted the fire brigade to check on the outcome; the firemen knew nothing about any fire; the same thing happened when, naturally, they drove back to the scene and asked around. The locals had seen no fire. But they did find out eventually that there had been a fire in that area twenty years before; an older resident had seen that fire and he described the scene exactly as the couple had seen it from the road.

Isaac Kirton

This is a Lincolnshire haunting from the doyen of ghost hunters, Peter Underwood. In his autobiography, *No Common Task*, he relates a tale told by Sir William Pike, who was a member of the Huddleston family, and the man in the tale called Kirton was actually a Huddleston. The story is from the Lincolnshire Fens.

In the early years of the nineteenth century, Kirton, who was a farmer with a strong presence in the Methodist community was riding along an area between Crowland and Fosdyke Wash when the weather took a turn for the worse. He was a long way from his destination when a really frightful storm broke out and he was being drenched. There was no choice but to stop and find somewhere to sleep for the night. Kirton saw that there was an old inn quite close, a place off the beaten track, with traditional, and very basic, accommodation. He went in and asked the landlady for a bed. The tale, written by Mary Huddleston in the late Victorian years, relates that it took some time for Kirton to persuade the woman that he really was in desperate need of a bed and some rest.

She finally relented and showed him to a room on the ground floor, down a long passage towards the rear. He rested, but there were some locals having a hard drinking session that night and he could not sleep until they had gone. He read, and waited. Then, after midnight, he fancied he could lay down his head, but as he did so, there was a rapping at the door. Kirton opened the door but saw nothing. Again he lay down, and again came the knocking. To his astonishment, he opened the door and saw three men facing him. One man spoke for the three, saying that they were three drovers and that a few months earlier they had come through the village from a fair where they had made some money. This is what the drover said next, according to Huddleston:

'The landlord, who is a crafty man, coveted our gold and murdered us in our beds and buried our bodies in the back yard that may be seen from your window there. If you will come with us we will show you the exact spot, so that the dark deed done that night may be brought to light and justice done.'

Kirton followed the men to the yard and they pointed to the spot where their bodies lay. Shivering with fear, the farmer then saw them dissolve and disappear before his eyes, but he had the presence of mind to stick his whip in the ground at the place they had located.

The next day, Kirton just had to find out if all that had been a real apparition and that the burial place was really where the drovers were. He found a local man who would go with him, bringing a spade, for a good payment, and the ground was dug, as Kirton watched. At first the man saw some clothing, and soon after that he shouted that he could see an emaciated arm, then a skull. Soon the earth was removed and there were indeed three bodies down there.

The landlord confessed and was carried off to trial. He was later executed at Lincoln, or so Huddleston says. This is a good story, but unfortunately there is no record of a hanging at Lincoln for such an offence; he may have been hanged elsewhere of course, but that is unlikely.

A15 Biker

The A15 is a deadly road, and it would not be any surprise to learn that there were ghosts along it, given that so many have died on its perilous stretch. As I write this, 36 people have died on the road so far this year (I'm writing in October, 2008).

But on the southern stretch, south of Lincoln on the Sleaford road, we have one of the most well documented apparitions from the county; by a particular bend about three miles before the Sleaford roundabout, and strangely close to a former Knights Templar settlement, a ghostly biker has appeared and held out a hand, begging for help. Some reports say he walks out into the road and tries to stop vehicles; others describe a figure in leathers with short-cropped hair, coming out towards the vehicle with a look of horror on his face.

The spot on the road in question is one of those tempting bends, appealing to bikers who get a thrill from a bend and a dip taken at speed. It seems almost certain that one such enthusiast was unlucky in that, and never drove home again one day. There have even been reports of this given on television, as on one occasion the programme *This Morning* accepted phone-in stories on the paranormal, and three people all verified this experience in that place.

The Grey Lady of Caythorpe

Around twenty years ago, Holy Cross House at Caythorpe, near Grantham, was demolished. The first part of the house had been built in the seventeenth century, but then in 1900, the local M.P. Colonel Royds, bought the house and he developed it significantly. That would make the home a very beautiful place to see and to be near, but there was something that kept people at a distance – the ghost of a grey lady.

Family members in the house recalled seeing the grey lady walk across the property, usually walk up stairs and then disappear into a bedroom. Unfortunately, there was a paranormal investigation at one time, but nothing was recorded that confirmed the tale. There was even a séance in the wing at which activity was most recorded, and one thing noteworthy happened there: the people learned that the spirit was of a murdered woman named Joan Bowling, and that she had been killed by a woman with the initials B.G. What is known with that in mind is that before the Colonel bought the house, it was owned by a Richard Bowling. At the séance, things turned nasty and the unwanted living guests were told to go away. Again, there is no murder recorded in the relevant time around 1850. Today, the site of Holy Cross House has nothing to memorialise the place and the dark, sad tale linked with it.

Clay's Light

Halton Holgate is a mile away from Spilsby, described by one traveller in late Victorian times as 'a pleasant well-built village.' In 1881 it had just 499 inhabitants. It has a great deal of charm – but it also has the story of Thomas Clay. Over twenty years ago a local wrote to *Lincolnshire Life* magazine to ask about the story of Clay, and she referred to her disappointment that she heard the bell toll for many residents' ...but had not seen Clay's Light.

The local tale is that when there is a funeral, the death has been foretold by the appearance of this light. Thomas Clay was a man who lived alone by the 'Fen' – a mile away from the church. Clay was the churchwarden in the years 1658, 1661 and 1662, and apparently he would walk to church for service in the evening every Sunday, but he would not use the road, walking over rough ground instead. When he died he left a direction that on his death, his coffin should be carried on that difficult route. Thoughtfully, he left some cash to pay the unfortunate pall-bearers to do this.

Understandably, the general feeling was that such a task was a waste of time and he was taken by road instead. But on the evening of the day when the funeral was to take place, a light was seen moving on the churchwarden's favoured route to church; the light then settled still on the church tower. Since that day, the story goes, when someone there is to die, the light shines over the home of the person destined to expire.

The village has another tale, told by a writer from Haxey in the 1980s who wrote that there was a ghost at High Farm and that it could have been 'exorcised by the fire that destroyed the farmhouse.' The writer says that the story began 'Just before the turn of the century, when the little hunchback who was troubling the foreman and his wife… gained widespread notoriety. My parents, who were living in Manchester, read of this in the national papers. By a strange coincidence, they went to live in the small farm close by. In my childhood I often heard High Farm called the 'Ghost Farm' but none of us ever saw the ghost…' The place was something of a tourist attraction back in the late nineteenth century, though what sightings there were of a hunchback is not on record.

Halton Holgate certainly seems to be a place where the unexplained has tended to happen. Research has so far not uncovered the story of the 'hunchback' and the burned farm, however.

The Rectory

In Fulletby Rectory there have been some accounts of an apparition. When the rectory was rebuilt two hundred years ago, a human skull was found in the rubble. Although the skull was buried in the right place – the churchyard – there it was again in the bricks the next day. This happened again, and so the next plan was to brick the skull inside the chimney.

The work then went forward and the new rectory was completed. But there was something restless inside that building, notably in a small passage; aspects of what happened suggest a poltergeist, because it was a noisy presence, and crockery was seemingly smashed in the kitchen, as well as other sounds being heard. But on investigation, there was nothing to see, damaged or otherwise at the location of the noises.

Servants at the rectory then began to feel the effects of the ghost among them, with the strange experience of having the bed sheets taken away; some of the servants understandably left the place. The research of Henry Winn relates that in 1854 the rectory was again rebuilt, and after that the ghost went, probably because the skull was taken elsewhere.

Miss Manby's Story

Twenty years ago, writer David Lightfoot researched what is arguably the strangest and most intriguing story gathered here. It concerns a Miss Manby, who had been an academic and Home Office intelligence officer. She played David Lightfoot a recording of a truly bizarre paranormal event.

Miss Manby was assigned to help a man called Peter Winthorpe, who was a Londoner being treated by a psychiatrist for his horrendous and frightening recurring dream of being a Lancaster pilot on a dangerous mission. On the recording, Winthorpe recalls how one night he was travelling home from Lincoln to Boston, after shopping; as he drove into a fog he was startled to see a black dog in front of him. He said it looked like a calf, in shape and size. But this is not a black dog story.

The man thought he swerved to avoid the beast and then he was aware of a policeman talking to him, but he sensed that the officer's clothes were not familiar. He was asked by the officer if he had been drinking, as there was a potent and sweetish smell in the car. He had taken no drink at all, and so the mystery thickened like the mist that strange night.

It was when Winthorpe realised that the smell was some scent he had bought for his wife that he understood he was not 'himself' – because he felt for the bottle in his top pocket and it had gone – but the oddest thing was that he was wearing different clothes. That was the trigger for the 'flashback' dream to begin, because he was seemingly a pilot in the RAF and about to gather with his crew to do a bombing mission over Germany. On the tape, Winthorpe said. ' What bothered me was why I knew it was the uniform of a Flight Lieutenant in the Royal Air Force while still wondering why it wasn't my three-piece suit.' Then, when eventually he drove away, he was at the wheel of an Austin 10. He was then in a flight briefing. He related ' In the locker room, I knew where to find everything but was still surprised to find that my heavy flying jacket fitted perfectly.'

The plane was to bomb Cologne (an odd irony when we recall the scent he had bought) and he said on the tape: 'The journey there was unbearably straightforward. Everything went well until we were right over the target area… and then that hellish kaleidoscope of red and black far below came into focus and I saw the cathedral. It was like a lovely toy on which a child has laboured for months to make out of matchsticks and we were going to stamp on it.'

Winthorpe followed orders, though, but as he moved the joystick to manoeuvre for the bombing, some force moved his hand in another direction. There was some anti-aircraft fire at them at the time and the crew thought he had deftly escaped that potential ruin. He knew that he flew the plane home, but then the next sensation was waking up in that roadside ditch, in the car. He was in the Metro he had been in after doing the shopping in Lincoln. Off to hospital he went and was of course interviewed by the police. An old ring had been found on him that he had never seen before; he was left with headaches and confused memories.

But Miss Manby's tale was not finished after the tape was turned off. She then said that under hypnosis, Winthorpe had given accurate details of the flight and all it entailed. But Winthorpe was born after the war, in 1949. David Lightfoot searched back into his own memory; as a Lincolnshire writer and historian he knew much about the events around the time in question, and he recalled a case in 1942 when a pilot who had flown twenty-three missions was found dead in an Austin 10 quite close to his air force base. Miss Manby then pointed out that the memory was true, but that the Austin had been driving towards the base, and so the pilot had died before he did the mission to Cologne. The crew of the plane had been certain that their familiar friend and skipper had arrived to fly the plane.

There were psychological explanations given, but it is hard to see how these particular facts can be explained away by cold logic. But there is a fascinating coda to the tale that raises the whole case to the level of total mystery: apparently some air-raid gunners in Cologne had made statements and one written report said that the fire-watcher at that period had recalled only one occasion on which he feared that the cathedral might be hit : he remembered seeing the bomber at that time swerve away, and he could see the pilot, with a man in a three-piece suit standing behind him. But the German added, 'And yet… he was somehow part of the pilot as well.'

As for the date of that particular raid on Cologne: it was on 6 January, Epiphany. David Lightfoot appealed for responses after publishing his article twenty years ago. There were theories and suggestions of course, but all the features of the tale suggest a template of the kind of paranormal narrative in which there is a certainty in all statements that forces were at work that were known to Shakespeare: 'More things in heaven and earth than are dreamt of in your philosophy.'

The Poet Laureate and the Stainby Ghost

J. C. Walter, writing in 1904, recounts the tale of a ghost at Stainby. He spoke to a former resident of the village, and the man remembered, as he said in dialect, 'Well, when I were young I lived in them parts and I heard o' one oftens. I never seen it mesen but I knowed several who did.'

The ghost was often seen at a spot around half a mile from Somersby close to the ash planting area. A waggoner who lived in Bag Enderby saw what he recalled as a 'misty kind of a thing... he knew it were there, and it flitted unaccountably' said the man at the time.

This ghost was not only noticed by locals: the tale reached the Poet Laureate, Lord Tennyson, who wrote of a farmer who was so bothered by this spirit that he harnessed his horse and cart and set off to escape the thing. Tennyson wrote:

> The farmer, vext, packs up his bed,
> And all the household stuff and chairs,
> And with his boy betwixt his knees, his wife
> Upon the tilt – sets out and meets a friend,
> Who hails him, 'What, are't flitting?'
> 'Yes, we're flitting' says the ghost,
> For they had packed her among the beds
> 'Oh well,' the farmer says, 'You're flitting with us too.'
> 'Jack, turn the horse's head home again!'

This story is linked to a whole genre of ghost tales, notably in Wales but also elsewhere, about the boggards who come to haunt a farm and will not go away. In the folk tales they always somehow stay with their victims, who have to try to sneak away while the boggards are otherwise occupied. Maybe in this case, legend mixed with supposed fact.

In Tennyson's poem of 1842, 'Walking to the Mail,' the treatment of the story is light-hearted: 'But his house so they say/ was haunted by a jolly ghost that shook/ the curtains, whined in lobbies, tapt at doors/

and rummaged like a rat. No servants stayed…'

The old man interviewed by Mr Walter had no doubts about the 'flitting thing' though. Maybe it's still seen today in that place.

SPECTRES IN THE HALLS
AND HISTORIC PLACES

Where there is the evident physical and topographical presence of the past, in the shape of buildings, gardens, artwork, walkways, vehicles and even artefacts from everyday work, there will be paranormal tales. The problem for the investigator in this context is that local myth will have mixed with the narratives generated by the heritage industry, and the need for every 'noble pile' with a long history to have a resident ghost. Across the country there are hundreds of such odd fusions of folklore and scraps of historical detail. But it has to be said that in Lincolnshire, the tales attached to halls, castles, abbeys and mansions have a solid track record of case studies, and in recent years various paranormal investigation groups have had field studies and vigils at a number of these. The results have been always interesting, though perhaps not always as sensational as might be expected.

Gainsborough Old Hall

The magnificent Old Hall near the heart of Gainsborough has been there since the mid fifteenth century, and the famous guests at the spacious manor house include Richard III and Henry VIII. All kinds of notables have been busy around its area and lawns, including John Wesley. But some of the guests have been from the other world, and most documented of these is a grey lady.

It is interesting to note that so many female apparitions on record are grey in colour. If we have a belief in some purgatorial stage after death, a limbo in which the spirit is held in suspension, as it were, then a colour such as grey indicates a closeness to a mist – a nondescript stage without colour, as if bold colours relate to actual physical vitality and then this recedes after death. A more down-to-earth reason might be that grey was a commonly adopted colour at certain periods in history. But whatever the reason might be, Gainsborough has its own grey lady and she may be a daughter of the Lord there who was in love with one of the Talbot family – not one of the celebrated and powerful Talbots in the fifteenth century and earlier, but a more everyday Talbot name.

The story is that she loved one of the Talbots of Torksey, and their lack of status was the problem, because the man she loved was only of a low order in those strictly class-defined times. He was a soldier and therefore not worthy of much respect and certainly not wealthy. The girl's plan to run away and elope with her young man failed, and the tale is told of her shutting herself away in the tower. From there it is easy to imagine the sickness and the pining away: at first, after her death, she was known to haunt the place as the 'Lady in White' – the other stereotype female ghostly image. But now those who report seeing her talk of her grey colour. Her most discussed appearance was in the nineteenth century when she terrified a workman.

Modern sightings have been few, but unexplained noises seem to be the way she communicates today. The tall building with its high ceilings and sense of bare, cold openness inside is conducive to such possible sounds from across the divide of death.

Thornton Abbey

The imposing remains of Thornton Abbey, not far from Barton, give testimony to the rapacious doings of Henry VIII, as it was one of the casualties of his depredations on the religious houses of that time. But the beautiful place has something dark inside – very possibly the villain Dean Fletcher, and also there could be the uneasy ghost of an abbot who was killed by Fletcher there.

In the late fourteenth century, the abbot, Thomas de Gretham, was enjoying a liaison with his student, Heloise. In a complex plot involving the abbot, a tough who was known locally as the Green Devil, and a stolen deed of land ownership, we have an awful tale of terrible punishment being inflicted on the abbot by Fletcher. Fletcher is reckoned to have felt the need to punish the religious man for 'lax living' and his particular form of punishment was to immure the abbot inside the walls of the abbey.

In the 1830s, workmen found a secret room where there was a skeleton on the floor, which turned to dust when touched. It was wearing a monk's habit and was most likely the unfortunate abbot. But there are other candidates for the identity of those remains. A report written in 1935 talks of a certain Walter Munton who was also spoken of as 'an evil liver' and the corpse may have been his. As with most of Britain in Tudor times, there was a threat of social anarchy most of the time, and these remains may well have been the victims of that supposed 'Green Devil' men spoke of at Thornton then.

The findings were reported in full in *The Gentleman's Magazine* for 1836:

> *'Adjoining the entrance to the chapter-house is an arched room, with pointed recesses for seats, after the manner of cathedrals. This apartment has no door, which is evident from the present remains, and was entered from the cloisters; by some, it has been stated to be the secret council chamber...'*

The editor added the note that the reporter at the time, a Mr Greenwood, had described the chamber in detail, but that 'If it was anything more than a portion of the cloisters, we cannot explain it; but the monks would certainly require no place of council more secret than their own chapter-house.'

Thornton Abbey.

In more recent times, visitors have spoken of being pushed or having heard whispers as they walk in the abbey; one correspondent has written that he 'felt a sudden sense of being overwhelmed with sadness' while standing there in the room over the arch, and that he had to leave the place immediately. This is backed up by other visitors talking of seeing shadows where there should be none and sensing movement in areas where they know that no other people have entered.

Harlaxton Manor

Harlaxton Manor overlooks the attractive Vale of Belvoir, and the house, at one time known at Grantham Castle, was built between 1837 and 1854 by Gregory Gregory, an art collector. It was sold in 1937 to Violet Van der Elst, a woman who spent many years campaigning for the abolition of capital punishment. Then between 1948 and 1965 the Jesuits ran the place. There is no doubt that Mrs Van der Elst was a powerful presence at the manor. She used to hold séances to try to make contact with her dead husband. These séances would be held in the library, a place described by one writer as 'sombre… with its twisted pillars from Italy and huge windows which were once covered with black velvet curtains.'

In the Jesuit period, there were frequent and unnerving disturbances at the manor, and there was an exorcism; a recurring ghostly tale is that of a young woman with a baby. The old story behind that was that many years before a young nurse had a baby on her lap by the fire, and she went to sleep, so that the child fell into the fire and was burned to death. The scene for these appearances is the ante room, and in that spot there have been all kinds of strange events, such as people arriving there for the first time saying that they heard the cries of a baby. Hearsay would have us believe that a hole in the chest of one of the decorative cherubs on the wall is something that testifies to the sad happening there.

The noted ghost hunter Peter Underwood once went to Harlaxton to give a lecture to some students, and he followed the talk by sleeping in the Clock Room, another paranormal location here. One of the students told Underwood of having terrible dreams, one time waking to see, 'what looked like a sub-human face close to his own, and sometimes, during the quiet of the evening, he had glimpsed a dark-robed figure in the room.' Other students who were there as part of the American University of Evansville, spoke of seeing that same robed figure and of

Harlaxton Manor.

seeing other shapes and figures in rooms. But Underwood ends his account of the visit on a positive note: ' Never shall I forget the first time entering the massive door, and Joyce and I finding ourselves alone in the sombre, shadowy, echoing stone entrance at Harlaxton...'

It could be that these unholy spirits were stirred from their repose by the questionable doings of Mrs Van der Elst, but the death of the child is supposedly something that happened in the Clock Room, and that tragedy had nothing to do with her séances – as far as we know. The questions remain of course.

Doddington Ghost

Doddington Hall is a charming and impressive country house a few miles to the north west of Lincoln. It has all kinds of historical interest, including a piece of Tom Otter's gibbet, as Saxilby is nearby, and Drinsey Nook where he killed his bride, is close enough to imprint the area with a sense of oppressive spiritual darkness and pain. But the ghost reportedly here at the lovely Elizabethan home is that of the Brown Lady, and she tends to be a benign presence.

The Brown Lady's origins are uncertain. What does seem to be the legend here is that she looks down on newly-wed brides from up above, and that the feeling is a good one, with no sense of menace. So much for the myth.

In modern experience, reports have been of shades and spirits in the gardens. The house has truly magnificent gardens with plenty of quiet places and secluded spots for a summer's day meditation – and that is just what one correspondent says he tried to do one day, but on waking from a doze, he saw a man in what he described as 'very olden day King Charles clothes.' The figure, he wrote, appeared to look at him closely, as if studying him, for a few seconds, 'and then it walked away towards the part where the horses used to be.' Was the man still dreaming? The obvious question has to be asked, but then another visitor has said that she heard talking as she walked along through the shaded flower beds, and when she turned the corner, there was no-one to be seen, for 'yards and yards.' Whatever is or is not there from the next world, there is nothing to strike fear into anyone. All supposed sightings or hearings have been innocuous.

Doddington Hall.

The Green Lady of Thorpe Hall

Some traditional ghost stories have clear links to both historical fact and to the balladry of literature. In that common interweaving of fact and fiction, the art of storytelling takes over and as time passes, it becomes more and more difficult to discern the real features of an original story. Such is the case with Thorpe Hall and its Green Lady ghost. We know that Sir John Bolle was knighted after the fight at Cadiz in 1587 and we know that he had been captured earlier in another Spanish campaign, but as to Green Lady, that is questionable.

The Green Lady was Donna Leonora, a Spanish woman who took pity on Sir John when he was imprisoned, taking him food and gradually getting to know him and of course, beginning to love him. When she finally arranged to free him by bribing his guards, her wishes could not be fulfilled because he was married, with a family back home in Lincolnshire. The main story focuses on Leonora staying in Spain and not being able to be with Sir John and to return with him, but time and imagination have created a tale of her coming over to England, seeing Sir John with his loved ones, and then taking her own life.

Thorpe Hall.

74

But there are other elements here, such as the fact that a place was always set for her at the family table, apparently up until the 1920s, and some elements of the story persist, down to the detail that some recent owners, according to Daniel Codd, saw a handprint by a gate at the place where the Green Lady moves from off the land into the places where she would have been near her beloved Sir John.

Normanby Hall Ghosts

Normanby Hall, a few miles away from the steel town of Scunthorpe, was designed by Robert Smirke, and is in 33 acres of parkland. Its attractions include a Victorian walled garden and some fascinating displays of life from another time, but the peace has been occasionally disturbed for some visitors. Although there is no established resident spectre, no Grey Lady or Black Monk, the reports of paranormal experience have been diverse.

One experience that seems to have recurred is the sight of a man on horseback who calls for help. One correspondent wrote that it was seen 'as I was walking through the woods towards the more open part of the land… I heard someone calling me and I turned, to see a horse galloping and the rider shouting to me. I thought it was real at first but then it disappeared from view, but strangely, as it came nearer – not as it moved away.'

Then there has been the sight of a woman wearing quite modern clothes. Reports say she might be a tramp, as she always looks poor and raggedly dressed, and she has been seen on the road leading away from the Hall, past the deer park. One witness wrote: 'She was wearing like the sort of clothes you see on *Dad's Army*…like a Land Girl maybe, but really scruffy. She walked into a hedge, or so it seemed to me.' That sighting was in daylight, in May.

The hall is unusual in that its history has not apparently given the modern researcher any stories of long dresses, old gentleman in black or laughing children at the place of a tragedy. There has been a happy story there. But still the times of the dead, and their mysterious locations, sometimes intercept our own place and our own sense of reality.

Farforth House

The ubiquitous Grey Lady appears yet again, and this time in Farforth, in the Lincolnshire Wolds. She first appeared in 1927, according to writer

Hugh Martineau, who has investigated this phenomenon. Over twenty years ago, Hugh Martineau spoke with the owner, and he reported that there was a stain on a floor upstairs and that there had 'always been an unpleasant smell of decay, for which there was no apparent reason, and it had defied all attempts to dispel it.' Could this have had any relation to the central story of the house – that of the lady in grey?

That story begins in 1927 when the Johnson family lived there. The lady was seen walking past the windows of the house, and was described as being like a Quaker woman; the child of the family once followed the figure, seeing her go down the cellar and then disappear. The story of the bloodstain was told at that time: that it would never be removed although it was scrubbed several times; both Mrs Johnson and her young daughter saw the grey lady walk by the window, always at noon. Then the Johnsons left – in the 1960s.

Hugh Martineau looked for historical roots for the tale, and he found that a man back in 1855 had been depressed after the death of his wife and had shut himself up in the room; the man had spoken about feeling that he was locked in Hell and that devils were tormenting him, that they would strap him into a chair they were making for him. He left the house, died in London, and was brought back for burial. Whether there is any link between the man and the lady in grey is not certain.

The people in the house over twenty years ago knew of a headless horseman seen in the area, and the story there was that a man was to be hanged on Gallows Hill but escaped, having his head cut off by the constable who chased him, and other tales of a ghostly man 'on a shaggy horse' persisted for some time in that area. But the lady in grey has the most convincing story on the record in Farforth.

FROM THE CASEBOOK

From the Casebook

As with my first book in this series, there is now an addition of stories from my own casebook. These tales cover both my own visits to places where alleged paranormal events have occurred and letters from and talks with correspondents after appeals in the press and radio for stories. The stress in this last section is on the 'everyday paranormal' and none of the following unexplained occurrences have ever been in print previously.

The Dog in the Pub

My correspondent recounted a time when she worked as a waitress in a public house in Billinghay. It was a busy place, with several bars and lounges to serve. On one occasion, because at that time the landlady had a dog around the premises, there was a black Labrador in the pub, and my correspondent would walk out to the rooms from the bar with drinks or food. The dog would get under her feet and she was sometimes likely to trip up.

Then on one occasion, she saw a large white poodle run across her path. She moved to dodge a collision and fell, stopping her fall with a hand. 'Look,' she told the landlady, I know you like dogs around the place… but you never told me about the white one!'

'What white dog? We don't have a white dog!' the landlady said.

'You have' the waitress said, 'I just tripped over it…'

'No, there is no white dog here. It must be a ghost!' The landlady was right.

The Ghost on the Bed

The letter came from a woman who had once been in bed when she felt that someone or something was in the room, and that uneasy feeling of dark expectation was fulfilled when, before her eyes, a part of the bed went down as if there was pressure exerted on it, just as if a person had sat down.

It was a room in an old house in which several people had reported seeing someone sitting in a chair in the corner; as there was a staircase there, and no space for a chair to be placed, that was odd. But some research established that, as the house was previously designed (back in the early nineteenth century) there was indeed a sitting room there, and the place in question would have been by a fireplace and inglenook.

The Soldier in the Field

Some years ago I interviewed a man who saw a redcoat running on Culloden Moor. The year was 1970, not 1746. It seems that soldiers are seen fairly often; naturally, their death has been bloody and violent, and so logically battle-fields are locations positively buzzing with paranormal activity.

A correspondent wrote with a memory of her grandmother's. The lady had been walking out in the fields on Ingleby Chase, walking with her little daughter. As they walked along the edge of a field, they both turned to look at the figure of a soldier – a figure quite clearly in the dress of a Roundhead soldier of the Civil War. He stood there, holding his horse as it drank some water. The little girl asked who the man was? The only answer, given in a tone of bewilderment, was 'It's a soldier love.'

The soldier was seen on more than one occasion. It would be logical to assume that this ghostly presence was perhaps the shade of a man who had been returning home from the field after the fight at Gainsborough, just a few miles away. On 20 July, 1643, Lord Willoughby took Gainsborough for the Parliamentary forces, standing in the way of the Royalist forces who were thinking they could advance from Yorkshire. The spirit of that soldier was arguably a man who had just experienced being part of a victory. The battle had been fought a few miles south of Gainsborough, so that makes sense with regard to the sighting.

The Ghost in the Tea-Room

In the Epworth tea-rooms at the garden centre, staff experienced a number of strange incidents over a period of a few months in 2007. First there was the startling find of a pair of bloodied gloves. They were in a locked cupboard, and no-one could offer any explanation as to why they were there and why they were bloody. After that there was the missing apron. This was always placed on a hook and then used or washed as the routine went on. But the spirit who was clearly having fun tormenting staff apparently took this apron away for a while. In fact, it never turned up again.

Finally, there was the recurring incident of the overall sense that when staff might be working alone, they were being helped or sometimes quietly watched. 'You used to feel that every move you made was being closely observed, as if a boss was checking that you were doing things right' one member of staff said. Was it possibly the ghost of a former manager of the place? No-one had any suggestions to make with that in mind.

Then it stopped. Was this a case of the haunter becoming bored with the haunted? It could be that the thing did not have the kind of response it craved from the living. But the staff were very relieved to be left alone to get on with their work.

Jesters-No Joke

In October, 2008, the news was out that the fancy dress shop at the foot of Steep Hill had some unwanted guests. Hazel Smith and her son have reported some very strange sights there, notably a hand coming through a wall and they have seen the ghosts of two children. The report was expressed with exactness: 'About a year ago I saw a hand slide through the wall, push a hanging costume and leave it swinging backwards and forwards.' That was given to the writers of 'This is Lincolnshire' – and it's not the only weird tale from the shop. Another testimony was that of Will Evans who had this story to tell: 'One day I took my sister up to the top floor, then nipped down again for something… She started really screaming. I rushed back up and she was staring into space. Back downstairs, she said she had seen two children.' The figures were seemingly wearing Victorian clothes.

Evidence is pointing to the fact that in Lincoln, the Strait and Steep Hill are a focus for all kinds of paranormal activity. It is almost as if there is a line of activity following the cobbles and the slope, where layers of historical time have settled and somehow kept a record of living souls across the centuries. There has to be some explanation for what had brought about such a concentration of phenomena in that small, circumscribed area of the city.

But in the meantime, tread warily when going to buy party clothes or toys. The jester may not be so wholesome and fun-loving. The remarkable aspect of the experiences there is that the details are so explicit, yet the supposed visual elements are so unusual: the bizarre often appears more convincing than the mundane, and that may be the case here.

The Haunted Lighting Shop

Cleethorpes Road, Grimsby, extends a very long way. Anything unexplained, any visitation from the other world, would have plenty of places to choose from for a haunting, but this entity chose a lighting shop. The owners called in paranormal investigators after a string of bizarre events.

The owners noticed something was not quite right there when first moving into the premises; bulbs were taken from lamps, over and over again, the shop alarm would be activated by the front door when quite patently there was no-one to be seen. When things were thrown, and therefore a poltergeist was suspected, the owners called in the Lincolnshire and East Riding Paranormal Investigation Team. There have even been visits from other experts, such as a shamanic pathwalker.

Conclusions are that the main suspect for the visitations is a violent wife-killer from the past, who enters the shop at certain times, but there is also another male spirit. The investigators have names for them – John and Tom. Of course, tracing the house or shop history could produce oher material, and that would seem to be the best course now. Steve Page reported on the trueghoststories.co.uk web site that such an investigation would be the next step, so we await results.

I have many cases similar to this in the case book, and the details about the male intruder follow a common pattern. In many cases such things are related to recorded data from archives. In the case of Grimsby, there are adequate reference sources, so from maps and newspaper cuttings there could be easy identification of the supposed murderer.

Screams in the Night

This is another tale from near Grimsby, and it refers to some events from almost two hundred years ago. In the early years of the nineteenth century, a plumber had been assembling a pump for a local aristocrat; he had been working late, so he had a good meal and some ale and set off home to Grimsby, on his mare. The first recounting of the story was in a local paper:

> *'He went through a dale and just when he had reached the bottom he came to a gateway. Suddenly he heard a most unearthly scream. He was terribly frightened though there was nothing to be seen, but the mare he was riding did, or at least it gave evidence of hearing something, for it dashed through the gateway and plunged along at a tremendous rate down the dale, never slackening its speed until it reached Laceby where it stood stock still, trembling in every limb.'*

Four years later, the plumber was working in that same neighbour-hood again, and a farmer came up to him, white with fear. He sat down and he said that he had been working by a gateway to fix a post and had come across some bones. He had asked the doctor to look at them and the medical opinion was that they were the bones of young woman, proba-bly in her twenties and that they had been buried about six years.

The plumber then told his story of what had happened in that very place. Research later showed that there had been an elopement at the place, Irby – or at least there was a supposed elopement. In fact, a bride-groom had repeatedly put off the day of his marriage to a local girl and then reports had said that the two of them had run away, over to Yorkshire. There was a letter sent to her parents, supposed to be written in her hand, but she was never seen or heard of again. The young man did come home, but said that he had not seen the woman, that they had been in Hull and had quarrelled and that she had left him.

But since that day there have been periodic reports of the scream. Walkers have talked about hearing someone seemingly in trouble, maybe being attacked, but on investigation, there has been nothing to see. This is one of those tales of restless bones and a possible murder – also a tale that once again reminds us of how sensitive animals are to the presence of the restless souls who have not yet passed over into the dark world of death.

A Poltergeist in Town

This is the most horrific and disturbing case in my own records, and I am withholding the names and places involved, as the present occupier of this property would not want anything specific to be detailed. Suffice it to say that this house is in a busy road in a North Lincolnshire town.

It started twenty years ago. The young woman in question came to me with a story half amusing but also not a little disturbing. She had two young children; her partner had left her. One night as she was watching television, she sensed that something or someone was in her kitchen. She picked up an ornament, thinking there was an intruder. 'I don't know why I did,' she said, 'I never would have used it.'

As she walked into the kitchen she saw a plate fly across the room and smash on the floor and then she heard a giggle. She thought it was a child who was playing a prank. After all, it was only a week before Hallowe'en. But there was nobody. Her children were tucked up in bed. She gathered herself again and sat down. Nothing else happened that evening.

About a week later she was cooking and the children were playing in the front room. The television was on, and she could hear music. But suddenly the music stopped and there was a crashing noise. She ran to the kids, thinking there had been an accident – and there had. The television was several feet from where it usually was, with the screen facing the wall. Her oldest daughter was laughing, but the woman was not amused.

Antics like this went on over a period of a few months. She persuaded her sister and sometimes her mother or friends to sit with her, as she was frightened of being alone. I went on just one occasion, and I can record that there was a chill like a giant fridge in a corner of the kitchen – but no fridge was there, just a shelf. I heard noises from upstairs, and the children were in the front room. But on going to look, nothing seemed to have moved.

Eventually, it led to an exorcism. There was no other option. Then the last I heard, she had moved house. The worst of all the experiences recorded was the voice. One of the most uncanny and disturbing features of such manifestations is the communication – often arms pinched or hands grasped, and also voices whispering. She went far enough away that, hopefully, the spirit grounded there in the dark house would leave her alone.

I have six such cases from research, but that has to be the worst. My own name for that presence was 'tormentor' – and I wouldn't wish that experience on anyone. What started as a case of laughs and jokes at the strangeness of the happenings turned into a living nightmare.

Girsby Lane Spectre

Eric Butcher doesn't like to think about what happened to himself and work work-mates back in 1963. It was something that would give a man nightmares.

Eric was working for Crowder's, a Horncastle gardening company at that time; he and three friends were travelling in a van, very early one day, as they were driving to work near Ludford. It was around five in the morning when the van turned off the A157 into Girsby Lane. Clearly, our minds are not at their most alert at that time, but what happened was bold enough at the time, and more than one pair of eyes were startled by it. 'It' was in view as the van went into a dip, over which trees arch over the road: the headlights were on, so there was no doubt that a white figure with its arms stretched out to them was plainly in vision.

The figure moved out, swooping low towards them, over the vehicle, touching the bonnet, and then stared in at the men before it moved away into the trees on the other side of the road. It's hard to imagine what reaction Eric had, but he knows that the driver slammed on the brakes and the men sat in a state of shock. Naturally, they thought at first that they might have hit someone walking there – but at that time, who could it have been? Maybe a tramp? But of course, when the shock wore off a little, Eric and his friends got out to look around, only to find no evidence of the figure's presence at that lonely spot.

Bev, Eric daughter, says that he is 'a brusque bloke, not given to fanciful storytelling' and of course, he feels uneasy when he tells that tale which brings back such a horrendously shocking experience, but the Girsby Lane spectre has to be one of the most powerfully disturbing visitations over the years in which the lanes of Lincolnshire have yielded up their restless dead. Readers may tread carefully along there after reading this story from forty-five years ago.

What Came Through the Street?

Thirty years ago, in Scunthorpe, something happened that was never discussed beyond a street in the town; it was something that you would not talk about beyond a circle of friends and neighbours, and yet as the years have passed, from time to time the people who experienced a mysterious event in the early hours of the morning still talk about this when paranormal subjects creep into the conversation.

As I was checking on this, I had the clearest account from someone who was a young mother at the time. Imagine having a toddler warmly wrapped up in bed and then being aware of something that came into the quiet – something disturbing but unexplained. The little boy woke up in tears. It had maybe been a bad dream: 'Something came through the room.' He was pacified and eventually went back to sleep.

But then, in the next few days, several young mothers mentioned a similar thing. In four homes, small children had all been roused from sleep, crying and unhappy, reporting a shape coming through their bedrooms. When checks were done on the timings of this, it worked out that there were just minutes between the events, as if the entity had traversed a certain long street in the town. I am not mentioning the name in case there have been similar events since. But what is clear is that it was more than a night wind, more than an uncanny series of linked nightmares. It was a visitation by something that did not mean well.

In historical records, even in medieval times, there have always been similar things, often related to belief in the Devil of course. But if we had to relate this phenomenon to anything previously noted as being similar, we would have to say that it was more like a sense of something evil passing that way, choosing to disrupt innocent peace. It might invite scepticism and people could talk of mere coincidence; I prefer to believe that the old folklore expressed in the famous classic ghost story by M. R. James, *Whistle and I'll Come to You*, in which inadvertent invitations and attractions are placed for evil to enter, are somehow relevant in this case. But on a more everyday human level, the children involved were also linked by a mysterious empathy, a sharing of an experience they could not express together, and not even in adequate words. Has this been repeated? I have no other records in my own files.

The Office Light

Going into the office first thing in the morning is something that millions of us probably do, a matter of routine, and this is such a perfunctory thing that the majority of us never notice much. But for one teacher in North East Lincolnshire this has been the case for some time – she very much notices something. In this case it is a light behind her chair.

She enters the room and immediately sees a light, perhaps a foot square, located behind her chair. The light is a blur, and concentrated. The teacher has applied logic to the situation, but come up with no explanation. The light occurs when there is no light source from anywhere else. It will be seen clearly, then, after a look away and a second glance, it will dissolve. The usual attempts to understand this have been tried: light, electricity, energy, heat, everything – but still it persists and it is without explanation.

More baffling is that the room is quite new: there is no chronological back-story to explore and research. This is no case of a suicide fifty years ago, or of a malevolence that insists on staying around. There is nothing frightening or unnerving: it just is there, and then goes.

Kitchen Antics

The kitchen is usually a place where we relax: we cook there and we often eat there. It is in some ways the hub of the family unit. We do not expect to be so afraid that we enter the room with a palpitating heart and a sense of impending dread and torment. But such was the case with a house in Brigg some years ago when I was contacted by a lady who experienced this for around three months – and then the entity in the room suddenly ceased to be there. 'I would walk in, wanting to boil a kettle or put a pan of potatoes on the go, for tea… and there would be a feeling that it was there, waiting' she wrote.

She was asked what kind of fear was felt; it was very much the kind of fear we feel when we have to go into a dark, enclosed space, and yet this would happen on a bright summer's day. 'It used to whisper… and I heard the words, "leave the place now!" she said. The important point about this was that she was on her own, and would always want to tell her family when they came to visit, which was every weekend, as she had three children all with their own families.

'You don't say anything… people laugh at you!' she wrote. This is totally understandable. After all, people would respond by saying that she was lonely and invented fears, emanating from the stillness of the house. But the ring of truth was in her letter to me, I am sure.

Back Seat Ghost?

Taxi drivers are used to odd happenings late at night. Usually this might involve drunks or people who are sick. For one Lincoln man we will call John, this was not the case – he had a visitor from some other place, from the land of the dead, he reckons. The first appearance was when he went for a job at about midnight and took someone home from a party. As he helped the man (who used a walking stick) get to his front door, he turned around and he saw someone sitting in the back of his cab, as there was a street lamp and this lit the back of the cab. He walked closer and asked what he wanted. 'I thought it was a drunk… maybe some kid' John said.

But as he reached the car and opened the back door, there was no-one sitting there. He reported that he had smelled lavender. 'Strange… why that? Maybe it was the ghost of a woman, and that was her perfume?'

It happened twice. The second time he was at home and it was dusk as he walked out to the car after calling in at home for a cuppa. 'I sort of stopped… froze. It was the figure again. I could tell by the outline of the head… it was like the figure had a sort of Elvis cut. Like a bouffant maybe, if it was a woman.'

After the second appearance, John would approach his car slowly if it was late or dark. But then time passed and there was no reappearance of the figure.

The Photo Across the Room

Jim's sister had died in a road accident. About a year after that, he had a picture of her framed and placed the picture on the window-sill of the lounge. She had died in Yorkshire, and here he was in Lincolnshire, maybe fifty miles away from the death scene. Then Jim had an interview for a job, and ironically, the job was to be just a few miles from where his sister died. The night before he was to go to that interview, something happened that he cannot explain.

The photograph jumped up into the air and flew across the room, landing by the door, so had travelled around eight feet. He immediately took this as some kind of communication, and linked it to the interview. He was right – he got the job.

'She was trying to tell me that I'd be okay... that she was there, sorting it out for me,' he said.

Photos and the dead provide a fascinating subject for paranormal research. Folklore, traditional beliefs and also lots of case studies present evidence that faces of the dead have a link to current reality at times at which a demand is made of them. Jim was still very much thinking of his sister. He knew that when he drove to the interview, he would go along the road where his sister died. Under that surface thinking about the interview, there was a sub-narrative, a communication with the dead, a need to hear from the other world. He certainly had a reply.

The photo has not moved since then. But there is one other odd aspect of this tale: he bought a rose bush in memory of her and planted it with four other bushes. The other bushes have never grown as fully as his sister's rose, and the strange thing is that her rose-bush flowers profusely on her birthday and on her wedding anniversary.

Bike Passengers Again

Some years ago there was a celebrated case in South Africa of a phantom hitch-hiker who stood on the highway wanting a lift. It was female, and she wanted a lift from bikers only. On at least three occasions, riders reported that she looked real, talked, got on the pillion, and then, at the destination, she was there no longer. The same story has come from Lincolnshire as well.

It happened near Grantham. A young man, reported to have been in leathers, hailed a rider from the roadside, and when the bike stopped, he smiled and said, 'Going into town mate... my bike's there.' The report was that this seemed odd, and that the hitch-hiker would not answer questions while riding. But then, as the bike stopped, 'I just knew that the man had gone!' The reported said that he must have been talking to himself for five miles, but still sensing that he had a pillion-rider.

'I never felt such a fool in my life,' he said, 'But I'm telling you now... Haven't spoken of this for a few years. You don't do you?'

He was right. We don't, generally, but my stories have only been possible because a reasonable number of people decided to write about – or sometimes talk about – their unexplained phenomena. In Lincolnshire we have a case of a county rather left out of the limelight when it comes to the more renowned unexplained tales, but these everyday stories, along with the established 'haunted houses' tales and legends, have demonstrated that the county has much more than the 'ghost walk' tourism the visitor might think is the sum total of paranormal activity there. The local and regional paranormal investigation groups are very active, and every week brings new stories.

The Window Watcher

I have left until now the most harrowing contemporary tale I have in the records. So many accounts of ghosts occur in desultory conversation, and we generally laugh or give a few safe comments that prevent the enquiry from going too deeply into the implications of what we have been told, but in the case of the truly terrifying experiences of Mr B. in his Lincolnshire home we have one of the most unusual happenings: one of those everyday paranormal experiences that can make the flesh creep.

Mr B. was asleep one afternoon in autumn – a quiet Saturday when he usually read the paper and dozed off. He was alone in the house, as his wife had gone shopping with a friend. We should let the story be told in his own words:

'Mr Wade, you are only the second person to whom I have told this story. Most people would accuse me of dreaming this, and some would say that I simply experienced a person who intended to burgle my house and hopped it very quickly, but believe me when I say that I came face to face with a being of some other reality – if in fact the thing was real in any sense…I woke up just as the light was fading. The paper was on my lap and the television on. But my heart jumped as I sensed someone outside. Staring through the window. I instinctively shouted and got up, to open the door and face the intruder. It sounds stupid, but I couldn't open the back door. There was some force holding it still.'

Mr B. scrambled around to the front door, aiming to run around to the back and confront the person. But he went through the kitchen as he did, and there he saw a face pressed up against the window. It was 'like a skeletal thing… but then there were red lips and suddenly a smile, like a deathly, emotionless smile…'

He gathered his courage and picked up a meat-fork from the kitchen, then ran around the back. There was no-one there, but as he stood by the kitchen window, he saw the outline impression of the face gradually disintegrate, 'just as the condensation goes after you breathe on glass.' He ran around the garden, looking for someone who might have jumped a fence and run off. After a while, after he had passed a neighbour but had been afraid to say anything, he returned inside and tried to watch television, though his heart was thumping, seemingly in his throat.

'I told my wife, of course. She was gob-smacked. But then she said I must have dreamed it. If only the marks had stayed on that window… If only I could have got hold of my camera…' It had been light enough for him to search for footprints in the garden and to look for anything that might have been damaged or might have taken some kind of imprint during the escape of the person, or creature – whatever it was. When pressed for more details, Mr B. insisted that 'The figure was not a human. God only knows what it was… but I know that the thing that looked in on me that day was out to torment me. I don't like to talk of it really, but you have to get these things off your chest.'

But of course, we don't do such sensible things when the dark world impinges on us. Mr B. told me this tale, and I feel privileged to have read it. I know instinctively that this was no dream. The very thought of someone or something staring at you, face pressed against a window, recalls the old House of Horror stories from the '70s, but I am convinced that there was nothing in that experience that was merely imagined, or that came from a dream.

If there is any substance in what Derek Acorah refers to as 'elementals' then this might have been one. In these instances, there is no voice, no touch, no sense of a being one may define and understand: just a powerful sense that something is there, exerting a force on the immediate location. Such things have been linked with witchcraft, and indeed Derek Acorah famously insisted that an elemental was present during the *Most Haunted* programme on the Pendle Witches (from the 1612 case). But Mr B. would, I am assured, not wish to go any deeper into things. He wants to let the matter lie untouched now.

The Visitor to the Pool

It may seem a strange sight, but three people, myself included, stood by a garden pool and stared at a footprint. That may seem odd, because one might expect a watery footprint next to a pool, but this was no swimming pool. Mrs F. had reported this as something that had happened on more than one occasion, so I had to ask more questions.

The pool was a home-made pool which provided a place for kids to paddle when they visited, but of course, there were rocks and stones, so frogs were tempted to join in. But normally, on an average day, nobody used the pool. That is, except for a mysterious visitor. This appears to be the only phantom paddler in my records.

'The first time I saw it, I thought we'd had an intruder,' Mrs F. wrote. The next time, she decided to have a vigil and sit up late to watch and see if there was someone from the neighbourhood coming in to have a paddle. But there was no such person, at least not until two in the morning.

The problem was – and it's the usual infuriating paranormal detail – the footprint, looking entirely like that of a male adult, would be there in the clayey soil for a while and then disappear. 'I never had the presence of mind to photograph it,' was the reason given. So I went to look, but it had been and gone.

I thought of other similar examples of this kind of thing, and I could find nothing in print. But I do recall a programme of *Most Haunted* on TV when the team went to study the *Queen Mary* in dock in California, and there was a similar instance. A footprint had been filmed by the side of what was now a dry pool: there had been no water in it for some time. I suggested that maybe the pool here in Gainsborough could be emptied, and we could then see if the print still appeared. No, that was asking too much. The puzzle remains: was this a mischievous drunk having a paddle? Or are we talking about a genuine paranormal experience? The case is still open.

Voices on the Stairs and Blood on the Photo

This story came from a phone call and I left it in my casebook for some time, not knowing whether to trust the source. The phone rang after an appeal for stories, and a lady told me that her house was haunted by something that was always on the stairs. She would walk upstairs and a voice would whisper in her ear, ' You hate this place… you hate being here…' it would say. This would happen fairly regularly. It seemed to be an instance of the spirit that wants the human out of the place, as if the location where the ghost is fixed is somehow a welcome purgatory, a place where isolation is needed.

I had experienced a similar thing when I was in my twenties and my father had died. A few weeks after his death, I was walking upstairs when I felt something touch my arm and then a voice said, softly, ' I'm here still, I'm here always…' I checked the clock and I realised that the time this happened was exactly the time that my father would get changed into his uniform: he worked as a security guard and would always get changed around nine in the evening.

I thought my caller would say the same, that she knew the voice and that it linked to some person they remembered. But no. Worse was to follow, and to this day I have no way of checking the story I was told. The second phone call talked about a photograph on the wall appearing to bleed. I was thinking that my caller was on medication maybe? Was this the kind of imagining we do after a few drinks? All I can say is that the person speaking seemed genuinely frightened and quite rational. She said that there was apparently a trickle of blood from the picture of her grandfather; it was a picture taken when he worked on the land, a farm labourer. There was no real knowledge of when or where the picture was taken.

I never heard the end of the tale, but I have checked on that type of phenomenon and strangely, kinetic action and photographic images provide us with the most challenging variety of paranormal experience on record. I asked the caller to let me know what developed, and the last communication I had was that the picture had been apparently hurled across the room, but strangely, the glass did not shatter. Once again, an open verdict.

I have met mediums who claim that photographs are the most productive items when attempts are made to use clairsentient contacts with the dead. Opinion is divided. All I can say is that my own experience at the village where the watercolour changed has made me want to know more. (see page 20). If images can change colour, then they can have kinetic action, I would suggest.

Conclusions

Lincolnshire is large enough to have its secrets and its hidden places; it also holds a host of hidden stories, long forgotten, and some of these have been encounters with the restless dead. There may be plausible explanations for many of the foregoing stories, but all I can say is that they come from written or spoken sources, and a few from my own experience. Other than that, the usual scepticism applies: we keep an open mind and we listen to the scientific explanations when they are offered. But other historians and folklorists have gone before and delved into stories across this fascinating county, and their stories have been tantalisingly inviting to the modern researcher and collector.

I feel sure that there are a thousand other everyday paranormal stories still waiting to be told. We all sense that something seen 'from the corner of the eye' or feel sure that a box on the table fell onto the floor when no-one was anywhere near it; we let these things pass and don't try too hard looking for an explanation, but these tales have been just a sprinkling of the accounts of what happens but is generally left unexplained. 'There are more things in Lincolnshire than are dreamt of in your philosophy' is my conclusion – with apologies to William Shakespeare of course. In a county so rich in highways and byways, it comes as no surprise that there have been bizarre experiences on those lonely roads and fens, wolds and farmland; so many of the old folk tales relate to horrible robberies and murders that happened over the centuries, that ghost-hunting notions would tell you just how many spirits around the place are downright malevolent, but surprisingly, not that many of the apparitions and spectres whose tales are told here have been thoroughly nasty.

A Return Visit

It is important is to revisit scenes of paranormal experience, and I determined to do that in this book, as I first wrote about a case in Epworth in 2005 and I felt the need to retell this. It concerns a woman in the village whose husband died not long before my first visit. She had reported going out to do some shopping, and on returning home, she got to the gate and felt sure that she saw him sitting at the kitchen table where he used to wait for her to make him some tea. He was not in the habit of making his own. She said that she could see his figure through the glass in the front door. Trembling with a mix of fear and excitement, she went to the side door and opened it, wondering if he would be there. He was not.

But I went, on invitation, to see the house for myself, and there I spoke with the woman herself and her friend. Both had seen things and heard things when they were together. They had seen the husband's favourite carriage clock move and be wound up, as he used to do when alive; they had seen the cushion in his favourite chair be pressed down as if something or someone was sitting on it. The wife said that on several occasions, she had heard knockings on the window downstairs – exactly where her husband used to knock when he was working outside and wanted something.

This is a case where I personally took some data and saw phenomena. First, I sensed that there had been a vegetable garden and I felt that I heard the knockings on the window. There was no vegetable garden there on the day I went, but that was confirmed. I also felt that there had been a dog, and that the husband and the dog spent a lot of time together in the small extension to the house. This was confirmed. The more I allowed the atmosphere to become prominent, the more I sensed that his spirit was there.

My update confirmed my suspicion, that there had been a settlement period – a purgatorial time perhaps – and that a peace had worked into the home, together with a recession of the need to see, to feel, the dead man there.

As was suggested in the first section, Epworth is a very special place when it comes to paranormal activity, and this case confirmed my opinion that there will always be phenomena observed and felt there, as if there is some kind of forceful epicentre where time crosses from the other world or worlds we only sense periodically. One confirmation always comes into my mind in these cases: that what we call 'ghosts' are phenomena that need a two-way channel, a need and a response working both ways, but perhaps we in this world do not understand how we operate the calling and the need for the other world, something often done below the surface of our logic-ruled lives. In all examples of this, there was never a clearer case than that of Harlaxton Manor and Mrs Van der Elst, a woman totally preoccupied with the reform of the capital punishment then in the criminal justice system; a woman deeply involved in wanting to speak with the dead. Her ghost is undoubtedly there still, and still restless for truths as well as for listeners. There is a two-way traffic in matters paranormal, and we are still working hard to understand how it works.

In Epworth, I had come to understand the potential in myself for seeing and feeling the presence of spirits, and this changed my perspective on the experiences I had read about and listened to, so many times. What happened was that I understood how our receptivity may be cultivated. I recall saying to the wife: 'There was a dog here. A small one… brown.' And she nodded to confirm this. Since then I have worked on that receptivity – an openness that may still be there, in spite of a basic scepticism.

In that visit to the haunted location in Epworth, I felt sure that my involvement in the communication that was taking place already between the two women and the spirit of the dead husband was somehow requested: as if a type of completion was needed. Perhaps, in the experience we call 'seeing a ghost' there is a glimpse into another way of seeing and another type of understanding; after all, there are huge elements in ourselves that present us with a mystery, so why should we expect a lucid explanation of a person from another time or place, beyond our current comprehension?

Even in the traditional paranormal tales – somewhere between folklore and legend – there is usually some substance at the heart of the tale that relates to something we know today, and still have reported every week. In the end, the stories from Lincolnshire may follow that pattern, going from local memory and oral tradition to something for the tourist events, but in the main, in this book I have done homage to the 'everyday paranormal' which is always with us, told over a coffee break at work or a Sunday dinner.

BIBLIOGRAPHY

Books

Bardens, Dennis *Ghosts and Hauntings* (Zeus Press: 1965)

Codd, Daniel *Haunted Lincolnshire* (Tempus: 2006)

Inglis, Brian *Natural and Supernatural: a history of the paranormal* (Hodder and Stoughton: 1977)

Langton, Edward *Essentials of Demonology* (London: 1949)

Lavater, Lewes *Of Ghosts* (Oxford: 1929)

Rawnsley, W. F. *Highways and Byways of Lincolnshire* (Macmillan: 1926)

Richet, Charles *Our Sixth Sense* (London: 1930)

Roland, Paul *Investigating the Unexplained* (Piatkus: 2000)

Rudkin, Ethel H. *Lincolnshire Folklore* (Beltons: 1936) Reprinted in 2003 by Old Chapel Lane Books, Burgh le Marsh

Simpson, Jacqueline, and Roud, Steve *The Oxford Dictionary of English Folklore* (OUP: 2003)

Sympson, E. Mansel *Lincoln: a historical and topographical account of the city* (Methuen: 1906)

Tennyson, Alfred *Complete Works of Alfred, Lord Tennyson* (Macmillan: 1895)

True Ghost Stories of the British Isles Bounty Books: 2005 (no editor given)

Underwood, Peter *Guide to Ghosts and Haunted Places* (Piatkus: 1996)

Underwood, Peter *No Common Task: the autobiography of a Ghost-Hunter*

Underwood, Peter *This Haunted Isle* (Dobby: 1993*)*

Walter, J.C. *Records of the Parishes around Horncastle* (W. K. Morton: 1904) (Harrap: 1983)

Westwood, Jennifer and Simpson, Jacqueline *The Lore of the Land: a guide to England's legends, from spring-heeled Jack to the Witches of Warboys* (Penguin: 2005)

Wray, Michael *13 Traditional Ghost Stories from Lincolnshire* (Caedmon Storytellers: 2003*)*

Wright, Dudley *The Epworth Phenomena* (London: 1917)

Periodicals

These have been generally useful, and many articles here draw on earlier research, so what has been passed down is a sequence of checks and questions about older stories, so that each re-writing brings new questions and maybe some answers.

Fortean Times
Lincolnshire Echo
Lincolnshire Life
Lincolnshire Magazine
Lincolnshire Notes and Queries
Lincolnshire Poacher
Scunthorpe Evening Telegraph

Specific sources are from these issues:

Lightfoot, David 'The reluctant Hero' *Lincolnshire Life*
    January, 1986 pp. 30-31
'Wayfarer' 'Legend of Gate where no Grass would Grow'
    Scunthorpe Evening Telegraph 31 March, 1954
Williams, Jared 'Some Lincolnshire Ghosts' *Lincolnshire Life*
    April, 1985 p. 28

Websites and internet sources:

Talk of the Town: Grantham 'Grantham's Ghosts' by Rupert
    Matthews Sept. 04
Petwood Hotel notes – at www.qype.co.uk/place
www.bbc.co.uk/lincolnshire/content/articles. This summarises the
    Scampton investigation
www.paranormaldatabase.com
www.trueghoststories.co.uk